omnibus presents the story of

# hear'say

by suzie russell

## OMNIBUS PRESS
London · New York · Sydney

Cover & Book designed by Phil Gambrill.
Picture research by Nikki Lloyd

ISBN: 0.7119.8956.7
Order No: OP48510

**Exclusive Distributors**
Music Sales Limited,
8/9 Frith Street,
London W1D 3JB, UK.

Music Sales Corporation,
257 Park Avenue South,
New York, NY 10010, USA.

Macmillan Distribution Services,
53 Park West Drive,
Derrimut, Vic 3030,
Australia.

**To the Music Trade only:**
Music Sales Limited,
8/9 Frith Street,
London W1D 3JB, UK.

Photo credits:
Front cover: Rex Features; back cover: LFI.
All other pictures supplied by All Action,
Big Pictures, LFI, Retna Pictures
& Rex Features

Printed by Printwise Limited,
Haverhill, Suffolk.

A catalogue record for this book
is available from the British Library.

Visit Omnibus Press on the
web at www.omnibuspress.com

## hear'say

**O**nce upon a time, anyone who went to their careers advisor at school and said "I want to be a Popstar" would've been sent away with a flea in their ear and told to buckle down and read a few good books. Now, it's the kids who can tell the teachers not to be "so silly". Because ever since the ITV launched the *Popstars* programme, the stairway to stardom has never been clearer.

Mixing fashionable 'reality TV' with a story reminiscent of the Spice Girls, the show took no fewer than 3,000 hopefuls, put them through their paces, weeded out the no-hopers (many of whom, to be fair, touched our hearts with their efforts) and ended up with the lucky fivesome who would walk into a five-album deal with Polydor Records. It was even being whispered that the five members of Hear'Say (as they were eventually christened) could be worth £3 million each by the end of 2001 – specially impressive when you consider the Spices took five years to gather their collective £20 million fortune.

It seemed incredible that by the end of April these five unknowns who, in January, could have walked down any main street in Britain without being recognised, would be sitting in the Top 3 with a double platinum (600,000-selling) album. But then, thanks to the magic of television, it would seem as if we'd known them all our lives – shared their struggles, hopes, fears and joy. Only time would tell how firm the friendship would be, but for now it was impossible to have a conversation in a pub, club, supermarket or playground without the same five names – Myleene, Noel, Danny, Kym and Suzanne – cropping up.

**The whole process of turning wannabes into musical megastars would unfold on our screens in a mere couple of months. The first of 12 episodes went out in early January as we were all recovering from the new year celebrations. This showed the 3,000**

**auditionees being put through their paces. By episode 3 (20 January), the focus had switched to Birmingham where the 175 selected for the second stage did their stuff. A week later, that number had gone down to 33, then 20, then 10. All had been welcome, the only stipulation an age range of 18 to 24 years, "so that once they were rejected they could be looked after by their families."**

Some music-biz veterans were outraged by the whole thing. Pete Waterman, the man behind such manufactured groups as Steps and the 'pop genius' behind Kylie and Jason, slammed them for being over-exposed. "They are a group without any intrigue, because we already know everything about them," he said. "Hear'Say's success at the moment is phenomenal. But where will they be by the winter?" Others, like Sir Paul McCartney, recognised that the five had genuine talent and wished them a thumbs-aloft "best of luck".

**The show combined the elements of three popular TV programmes: *Big Brother* (in its fly-on-the-wall element), *Stars In Their Eyes* (the glittering prize on offer) and *The Weakest Link* (with only the strongest surviving). With that addictive formula, how could it possibly fail? The idea had already been run in Australia, where all-girl five-piece Bardot had topped the charts first time out: in fact, they were so successful that one in sixteen Australians were reckoned to own their debut album.**

The beauty of the Popstars show is that, though there were far more 'weakest links' than winners, we would remember even them with affection. Take Darius from Glasgow, whose version of Britney Spears' 'Baby One More Time' was positively unforgettable, was maddeningly cocky and positively demanded celebrity status, while another Scotsperson Claire was unanimously acclaimed as a hugely talented singer even though she was the opposite end of the scale from the thin-as-a-rake identikit girl-group type.

**Robbie Williams' 'Angels' was a popular solo audition song, and was interpreted (or murdered, if you prefer!) in several different ways, while Simon and Garfunkel's**

**'Bridge Over Troubled Water' and the Mamas & The Papas' 'Monday Monday', two pop classics from the past used to see how different individuals' voices blended, proved so popular with viewers of all ages that they would be revisited for the album.**

Villain of the piece was chief judge 'Nasty Nigel' Lythgoe, a TV boss who wasn't afraid to say what he thought – and polish it up for the cameras. Sample comment: "Nice performance. I'm sure the tune is in there somewhere." Nigel went on to land a lucrative new job opportunity with a rival channel after the show while fellow judge Nicki Chapman snapped up a post with Simon Fuller's 19 Management. (He, in case you'd never heard of him, is the creator of the Spice Girls and S Club 7, and arguably the man who did all this first.) So who says there were only five winners?

The tension mounted week by week, culminating in the so-called Green Mile which each of the contestants had to walk to find out if they were destined to progress or whether they would fall by the wayside. On the way to learn their fate, they'd receive feedback from the judges on how they'd done... and you'd best believe more than a few swiftly hidden tears were shed along the way. Certain false trails were introduced to lead us off the scent. A gorgeous brunette called Myleene was criticised for being late and even – horror of horrors – missing an audition. No chance for her, then! Then there was Noel, the shy Welsh lad who had to have his arm twisted to attend. Definitely lacks the drive to succeed, we sniffed. Wrong!

Feisty northerner Kym, meanwhile, stayed up late partying in her hotel room with the lads, and found the next day her voice had seized up. Undaunted, she picked herself up off the floor to sail through the group audition. Wrong again! What no-one knew at that stage (including the TV company) was that the 24 year-old Lancashire lass had two kids at home! That, and many other surprises, were yet to unfold...

With nine audition centres, it's not surprising the winning quintet had been brought together from all corners of the country. Londoner Danny and East Anglian beauty Myleene had attended the London auditions, while Lancashire lasses Suzanne and Kym made the short trip to Manchester. The other centre to yield a winner was Cardiff, where Noel was discovered. Polydor Records A&R Manager (talent scout) Paul Adam was delighted at the standard of the auditionees. "The surprising thing about the whole project," he remarked, "has been the quality of the talent. I could have made a dozen bands from the contenders I saw – and that means the five we have in the final band are true stars."

Uniquely, Episodes 6 and 7 were broadcast on the same day. The first gave us our last chance to choose from the 10 finalists before ten became five and the judges were given the task of meeting the chosen ones' parents and telling them to expect fans camping on their front gardens. Episode 8 was broadcast from the secret location that was the Popstars house while Episode 9 saw them meet the star-making machine for the first time.

The switch from weeding out the no-hopers to following the career of the winning fivesome cut down on the drama, but at the same time gave the show a new dimension. As Polydor's Paul Adam put it, "This is the stage when the public start rooting for performers. The humiliation aspect of the entertainment will hopefully be replaced with affection for individuals." *Heat* magazine agreed. "Is it as good now we can't entertain ourselves with tone-deaf fools at auditions?" they asked. The answer was "Yes – just a little different, that's all."

The TV screening had started off about six weeks behind 'real life' and, though this time lag caught up as the series went on, the delay inevitably meant secrets had to be kept. The tabloid press were understandably hungry to reveal all – and their first task was finding the north London 'Popstars House' where the winning members were getting to know each other. Not even the closest family of the five were let in on the location, as Suzanne revealed. "Even our parents didn't know where we lived. If anyone rang the doorbell we'd run away screaming."

**So much had to be organised before the scheduled March release of their first album. Which track would be the best single? What dance routines would they go for? What would their image be? Who would say what to the press? The clock marched relentlessly on, and we kept our fingers crossed as the stars who'd found a way to our hearts aimed for the charts.**

While the five were being put through their paces and groomed for stardom in record time, a backroom team had already been assembled for them to work with, each member experienced in their field. Their manager would be Chris Herbert, one of the team that had discovered Five, while the writers and producers lined up to work with the band included the duo of Pete Kirtley & Tim Hawes (who'd write the first single with Alison Clarkson, alias Nineties starlet Betty Boo) and Spice Girls/911 collaborator Elliott Kennedy. Later on arrived Ray 'Madman' Hedges, who'd been in on Boyzone's rise to fame and fortune.

**As February turned into March and the first sunshine of spring poked from behind the clouds, we followed the famous five as they took their first giant steps to stardom. First, though, a change of location – to Norway, for a session with the Stargate writing and production team which had worked its pop magic on acts like N'Sync and Five. As the public weren't to see this on their screens for some weeks yet, the group members were secretly smuggled out of the country like wanted people – which, in a way, they were!**

Next came the choice of name. Here, the TV company Granada was either clever or got found out, as they had secretly registered a website for Inner Spin. This domain name was leaked to an eager press… who were therefore dumbstruck when the five were unveiled as Hear'Say! The apostrophe was clearly all-important – and, even more importantly, the guys and girls were all happy about their new label.

So who were the successful singers, and what had driven them to succeed? One thing was for sure, they all had very different backgrounds. They ranged in age from 19 (blonde, bubbly Suzanne Shaw) to 24 (mother of two Kym Marsh), while their showbiz experience to date was equally diverse. 22 year-old Myleene Klass had played piano and violin from age four, turned down a place at Cambridge University studying music and had recently been a backing vocalist for top pop stars Cliff Richard and kd lang. By comparison, Londoner Danny Foster, just a year younger, had hardly started. It wasn't until he entered a talent contest in Tenerife at age 15 that his family even knew he could sing, while he'd spent more recent years DJ-ing in London clubs as much as performing in his own right.

**Twenty year-old Noel Sullivan from Cardiff was certainly experienced in singing – but as part of a male voice choir in his native Wales! He'd formed a pop vocal group with some of his younger choirmates called Only Men Aloud – but was more than happy to relax that rule to get a place in the final five. He'd been pushed by a family friend to attend auditions, and was certainly far from the loudest member of the group... but they say the quiet ones have hidden depths!**

Kym had been to stage school in Liverpool after showing early singing promise, but teenage parenthood seemed to have put a stop to such ambitions. She never gave up hope, though, despite having sung with a number of bands that failed to make it. Suzanne, like Kym a Lancashire girl, had cut her performing teeth as part of an Abba tribute band called the Right Stuff. Her outgoing, sometimes outrageous personality made her a natural – though the hair extensions she adopted as a new image before the band was unveiled caused more arguments among fans than anything else!

**It wasn't long before the tabloid press were searching for any 'exclusive' angle they could find – ex-lovers, schoolfriends, whatever. And Kym was first in the firing line for being a single parent, a secret she'd revealed to 'Nasty Nigel' on screen to a surprisingly sympathetic reception. How dare she leave her children to pursue her selfish dreams, thundered the guardians of Britain's morality? She sensibly suggested it was no different to a man going off to work on an oil rig to keep up his family's standard of living – and besides the children were in her parents' loving care.**

Myleene's 'skeletons' were an allegedly two-timing male model boyfriend (the pair are still together, so that appears to have been unfounded) plus a part in a satellite TV 'internet diary'-style programme *The Doll's House* (she sensibly opted out before the show turned steamy). 'Naughty' Noel had apparently supplied backing vocals for female impersonator Ceri Dupree as she played Tina Turner and Shirley Bassey, while Suzanne was alleged to have pinched someone's boyfriend (not literally!) while doing her Abba impersonations. Only Danny escaped the scandal-mongers... but to be honest, nothing in this tabloid tittle-tattle ever looked likely to split up the dream team.

With 12 million viewers hooked on their weekly dose of Popstars, it was always odds-on that Hear'Say's first single would hit the top – and so it proved. 'Pure And Simple' was the song – and its rise to the top was just that. Its first-week UK sales were the highest of any debut single ever, leaving it as Number 3 behind Band Aid (1984) and Elton John's Diana tribute (1997). And when the album, simply entitled *Popstars*, hit the record racks a fortnight later, sales were similarly spectacular. Debuting at Number 1, it held off the likes of the Manic Street Preachers and The Bee Gees to sell 100,000-plus in its first three weeks on the chart. Only Dido, whose *No Angel* album had been around all year, could claim a higher total, but Hear'Say had her firmly in their sights.

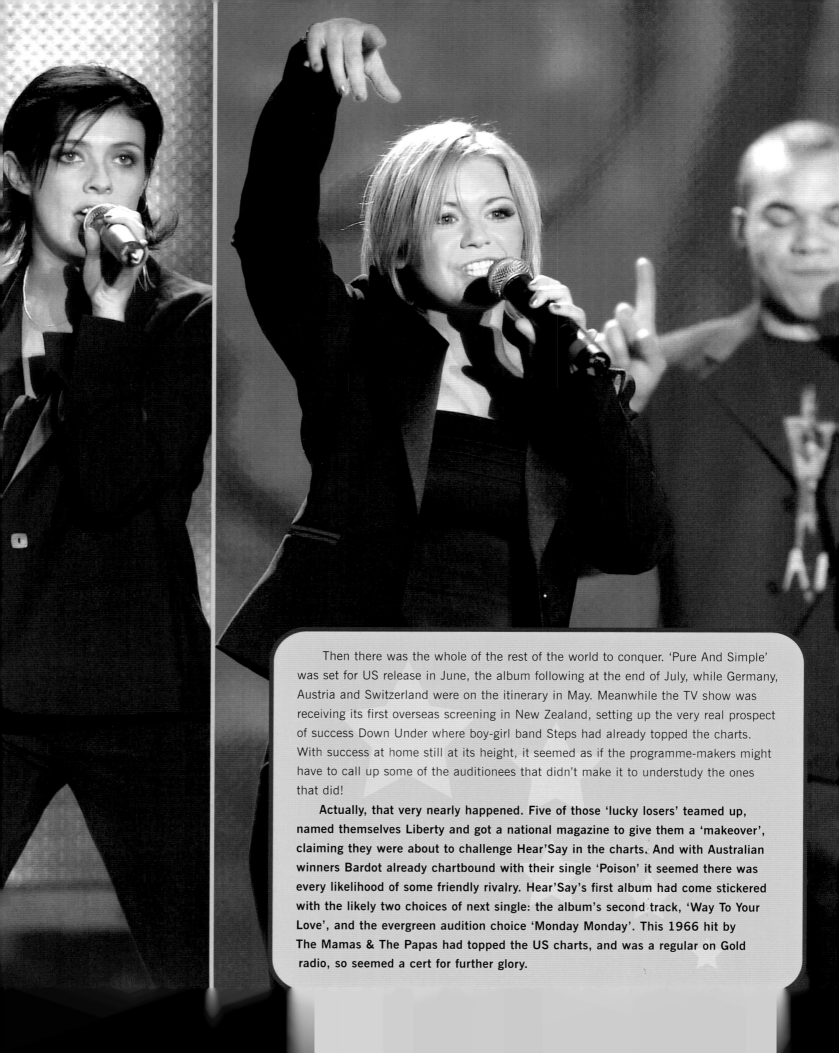

Then there was the whole of the rest of the world to conquer. 'Pure And Simple' was set for US release in June, the album following at the end of July, while Germany, Austria and Switzerland were on the itinerary in May. Meanwhile the TV show was receiving its first overseas screening in New Zealand, setting up the very real prospect of success Down Under where boy-girl band Steps had already topped the charts. With success at home still at its height, it seemed as if the programme-makers might have to call up some of the auditionees that didn't make it to understudy the ones that did!

Actually, that very nearly happened. Five of those 'lucky losers' teamed up, named themselves Liberty and got a national magazine to give them a 'makeover', claiming they were about to challenge Hear'Say in the charts. And with Australian winners Bardot already chartbound with their single 'Poison' it seemed there was every likelihood of some friendly rivalry. Hear'Say's first album had come stickered with the likely two choices of next single: the album's second track, 'Way To Your Love', and the evergreen audition choice 'Monday Monday'. This 1966 hit by The Mamas & The Papas had topped the US charts, and was a regular on Gold radio, so seemed a cert for further glory.

The urge to see their screen idols in the flesh made Hear'Say the biggest draws in pop. With 500 expected at Milton Keynes for a single signing, the shopping centre had to close when 2,000 turned up, while a planned appearance at the vast Bluewater mall in Kent was called off when crowd safety couldn't be guaranteed. They'd made their first live appearance at the Sound Republic Club in London just before singing at the Brits, but the real test would come in August when they kicked off their debut UK tour.

**Five extra dates were immediately added to the eight already announced after the opening show, at Cardiff Arena, sold out within an hour, while four others put up the 'house full' signs within two hours of going on sale. They'd also been lined up to follow in the footsteps of Steps, Five, Louise, Samantha Mumba and Kylie Minogue by performing at performing at the Mardi Gras outdoor festival in London's Finsbury Park in late June in front of 85,000 people – an experience sure to cure stage fright if nothing else!**

Meanwhile, it was suggested that the Labour party wanted to use 'Pure And Simple' as an election anthem because of both its inspiring sentiments and the group's 'young and ambitious' vibe. Apparently, they'd gone off first choice S Club 7's 'Reach'! But our heroes said thanks but no thanks, a spokesman confirming "Hear'Say do not back any political parties." It was clear that, to the envy of Blair, Hague and the rest, they already had the nation's vote.

**With 15 album tracks to choose from, each a potential single, it seemed 2001 would remain the year of Hear'Say. News also came that they planned to cover a Wham! hit as part of *80s Mania*, a TV programme celebrating the decade. And, according to bookmaker William Hill, "all that could stop them having this year's Christmas Number 1 is something like Bob the Builder."**

So barring a Bob revival or a late burst from Mr Blobby, all seemed set for Myleene, Kym, Noel, Danny and Suzanne to keep the pop flag flying for many months, if not years, to come. Let's let Noel have the last word – and maybe, just maybe, let slip the secret of why Hear'Say have attracted us. "They've all got the kind of qualities you'd like in yourself," he says of his fellow members. "If you could roll them all into one, they would be the perfect person. They are my new best friends and work colleagues, and I couldn't have wished for a better bunch." That's purely and simply it!

LIFELINES

hear'say

# KYM

**FULL NAME:** Kimberley Gail Marsh

**WHEN BORN:** 13th June 1976

**WHERE BORN:** Merseyside

**ZODIAC SIGN:** Gemini
(a restless seeker after new sensations)

**HEIGHT:** 5 ft 4 in

**COLOUR OF HAIR:** Brown

**COLOUR OF EYES:** Hazel

**FIRST RECORD BOUGHT:** 'Hangin'
Tough' (New Kids On The Block, 1989)

**LIKES:** The Simpsons, her children

**DISLIKES:** Eminem

**FAVOURITE SINGER:**
Andrea Corr, Karen Carpenter

**FAVOURITE BAND:** Five

**FIRST PERFORMANCE:** Age 10 in
a club in Wigan, singing 'Living Doll'

**PREVIOUS EXPERIENCE:** Groups
Mother Earth, Solar Stone, Sebatu

**AUDITION LOCATION:** Manchester

**DESCRIPTION:** Everyone agrees Kym
is the Mother of the group, the one
who protects them against criticism and
the one they come to for a cry on the
shoulder when it all gets too much.
"She's very sure, but also very sensitive,"
says Myleene.

# NOEL

**FULL NAME:** Noel John Sullivan

**WHEN BORN:** 28th July 1980

**WHERE BORN:** Cardiff

**ZODIAC SIGN:** Leo (warm, affectionate, loves to be the centre of attention)

**HEIGHT:** 6 ft 1 in

**COLOUR OF HAIR:** Black

**COLOUR OF EYES:** Brown

**FIRST RECORD BOUGHT:** 'Would I Lie To You' (Charles & Eddie, 1992)

**LIKES:** Family life, cooking

**DISLIKES:** Bad boy bands

**FAVOURITE SINGER:** Tom Jones

**FAVOURITE BAND:** Stereophonics

**FIRST PERFORMANCE:** At school (he got drama and music A-levels)

**PREVIOUS EXPERIENCE:** Choir, own group Only Men Aloud

**AUDITION LOCATION:** Cardiff

**DESCRIPTION:** The Stephen Gateley of Hear'Say, his "brown eyes and dazzling smile will probably help him secure a place in the line-up" wrote *Heat* magazine before the final five had even been selected!

# MYLEENE

**FULL NAME:** Myleene Angela Klass

**WHEN BORN:** 6th April 1978

**WHERE BORN:** Norfolk

**ZODIAC SIGN:** Aries (raunchy, passionate and impetuous)

**HEIGHT:** 5 ft 6 in

**COLOUR OF HAIR:** Brown

**COLOUR OF EYES:** Brown

**FIRST RECORD BOUGHT:** 'Love Shack (The B-52's, 1990)

**LIKES:** Chocolate, bed

**DISLIKES:** Ironing, spiders

**FAVOURITE SINGER:** Britney Spears, Kylie Minogue

**FAVOURITE BAND:** Five

**FIRST PERFORMANCE:** Amateur dramatics when still small. Previous experience: Session singer for Cliff Richard

**AUDITION LOCATION:** London

**DESCRIPTION:** Kym describes her as the brains of the band, the friend she'd call if ever she got on to *Who Wants To Be A Millionaire*. Cool, calm, collected and (very) talented – that's Myleene!

# SUZANNE

**FULL NAME:** Suzanne Christine Shaw

**WHEN BORN:** 29th September 1981

**WHERE BORN:** Bury

**ZODIAC SIGN:** Libra (charming and charismatic with two sides to her nature)

**HEIGHT:** 5 ft 2 in

**COLOUR OF HAIR:** Blonde

**COLOUR OF EYES:** Blue

**FIRST RECORD BOUGHT:** 'The Loco-Motion' (Kylie Minogue, 1988)

**LIKES:** Phoning people, animals

**DISLIKES:** Housework, heavy metal music

**FAVOURITE SINGER:** Madonna

**FAVOURITE BAND:** Abba – who else?

**FIRST PERFORMANCE:** Played Molly in the musical Annie at age four

**PREVIOUS EXPERIENCE:** Sang in an Abba tribute group

**AUDITION LOCATION:** Manchester

**DESCRIPTION:** Kym reckons Suzanne is "a bit of everything", while Noel calls her "loveable and wacky". Certainly she's always on the phone – so, a tut-tutting Kym reckons, "her brain's going to be shrivelled." Now that's what we call a hang-up!

# DANNY

**FULL NAME:** Daniel Paul Foster

**WHEN BORN:** 3rd May 1979

**WHERE BORN:** London

**ZODIAC SIGN:** Taurus
(passionate yet practical)

**HEIGHT:** 5 ft 10 in

**COLOUR OF HAIR:** Brown

**COLOUR OF EYES:** Blue

**FAVOURITE RECORD:**
'Ain't No Stoppin' Us Now'
(McFadden & Whitehead, 1979 -
the year he was born!)

**LIKES:** Sport

**DISLIKES:** His height

**FAVOURITE SINGER:** Stevie Wonder

**FAVOURITE BAND:** Damage

**FIRST PERFORMANCE:** On holiday,
age 15, singing 'La Bamba'

**PREVIOUS EXPERIENCE:**
On the London pub and club scene

**AUDITION LOCATION:** London

**DESCRIPTION:** Noel says he's like
a big brother, really strong but with
the same insecurities about fame.
So, a mixture of the tough and the
tender, then.

hearsay

"This is the most manufactured band ever but we are five talents. If only this process had been done with other bands we wouldn't have to put up with so many rubbish one-hit wonders and naff groups."

## NOEL

"The hair extensions were my idea – I suggested them. Unfortunately when the world saw them at our press conference I was having a bad hair day... they're totally impossible to control. I've got different ones now – they're shorter."

## SUZANNE

"The music industry should be shaking in its boots. We are putting pop back where it belongs – live and on the stage. People turn their noses up, but now they know we can sing!"

## MYLEENE

"I always felt that my kids deserved more. I tried out for Popstars because I didn't want to be sitting in Wigan on income support for the rest of my life."

## KYM

"There's no lead vocalist, the songs use all of our five voices equally. It's very good pop music, I think people are going to be really surprised."

## DANNY

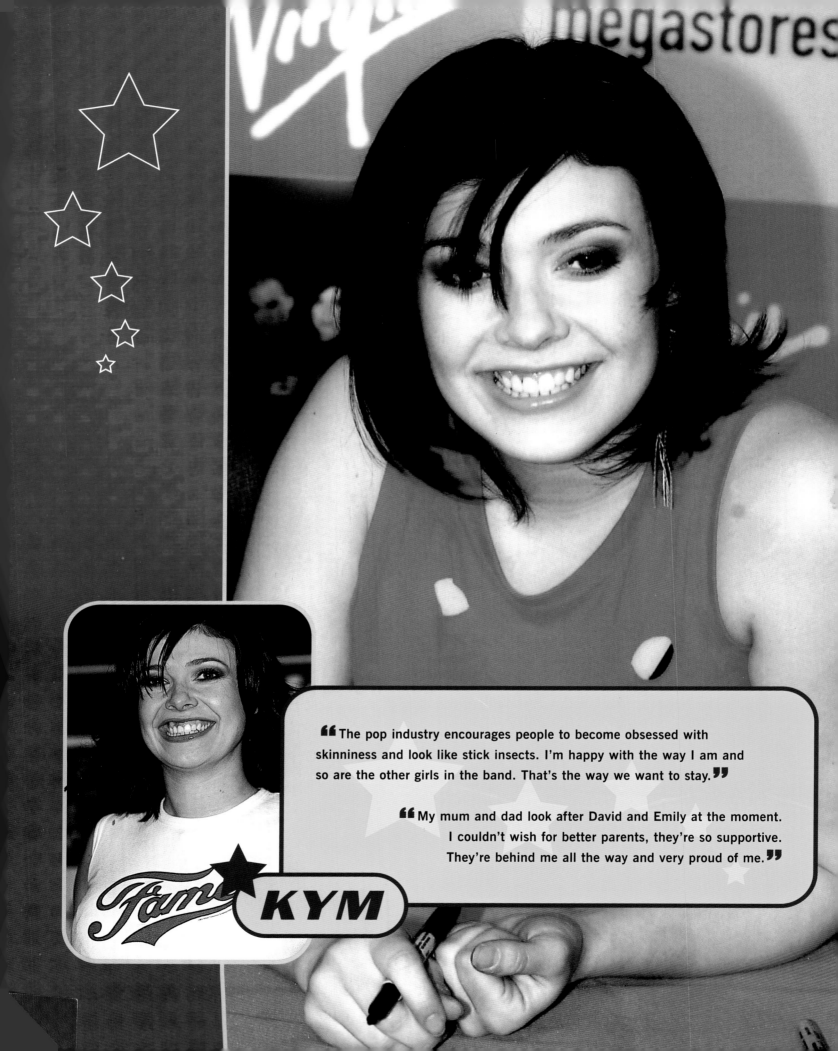

**" The pop industry encourages people to become obsessed with skinniness and look like stick insects. I'm happy with the way I am and so are the other girls in the band. That's the way we want to stay. "**

**" My mum and dad look after David and Emily at the moment. I couldn't wish for better parents, they're so supportive. They're behind me all the way and very proud of me. "**

KYM

"We're not listening to all the hype. We really don't have a clue about what's going on out there. We're still in our little Popstars bubble working 24 hours a day..."

## NOEL

"Could we be bigger than the Spice Girls? We've only just got together, we've got to see how it goes. My ambition was to be in a pop band, so now I want to work hard to make us successful."

## SUZANNE

"Kym always wants to watch a video last thing at night, then she'll pass out and I'll end up watching it on my own while she snores! She's a morning person, I'm an evening person."

## MYLEENE

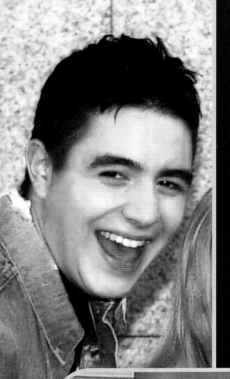

"I would love to meet Madonna. She's always been an idol of mine. I'd also love to meet Anastacia. She's got a really good voice."

**SUZANNE**

"Noel's the impressionist, always making you laugh. He even takes me off now – the Cockney accent! I couldn't ask for anyone better in the band. I'm the quiet one."

**DANNY**

"Noel is the comic of the band and very, very witty. If he didn't make it as a pop star he could always be a comedian. He makes you feel better and is the first one for a hug if you're not feeling yourself."

**KYM**

## NOEL

"We were put in a house together, sealed off from the outside world and that whole time was kind of surreal. The way we bonded was really special. We had to build up a strong friendship."

"We talk about everything and we said from day one it was never going to be about me, it's just we. I'm still waiting for the day we have a big blow-out, but we've been getting on fantastically so far."

**"** We're still normal. We eat pizzas at midnight and wake up with spots on our faces. We do normal things and that will never change. I've never met four easier-going people in my life – the judges chose well.**"**

**"** Even when I was training in opera, I wanted to be a pop singer. The classical groups said it was a waste and that it would strain my voice. But locking myself in a room for eight hours a day wasn't for me.**"**

## MYLEENE

" Myleene has a good business head on her shoulders, which performers often don't have, so that's great. She's very grounded. She deals with the lawyers, the TV company and the record company. "

**NOEL**

" I stacked shelves at Marks & Spencer at night and went to auditions during the day. I wanted to give it a go – and I did. I could go back to working as a cleaner if I had to... but I don't think I will! "

**DANNY**

" I don't really worry about whether or not we're taken seriously. Yes, we were introduced by a television programme, but look at S Club 7. They did it and they've moved on. They're far more credible now... "

**KYM**

**"** We don't have to sing anything we don't want to sing. If we don't like it we don't do it – it's as simple as that. Same with the image. We discuss what we like and the stylist works round that. **"**

### KYM

**"** The critics go on about our looks our training, what we're eating. They just won't focus on our singing. We worked so hard to get the sound together, to get our voices out there. Looks? Clothes? The criticism has to be about music, surely? **"**

### MYLEENE

**"** Suzanne is very balanced. One minute she's quiet, the next she can be so funny. She's quirky and sweet – and always on her phone, which plays the Flintstones tune. **"**

### DANNY

"When I'd heard I'd won I was just thinking about the music and the fame and how I was going to cope. Until I walked through the airport coming back from the recording sessions in Norway I had no idea how big the whole thing had got."

"Which member of Hear'Say am I? I don't know, how about Blondie Hear'Say? No, ignore that, I'll be Mobile Hear'Say cos I'm never off my phone!"

> "The thing I'm most looking forward to about being a pop star is hearing our songs on the radio, without a doubt! Going to swanky parties and not having to queue for clubs will be nice too."

> "I was really worried that the final five in the house would be performing for the cameras, but thankfully everyone is really natural and just themselves."

**DANNY**

> **I** I was a bit upset when the judges said I was always late because that wasn't entirely true. They just said that for the TV. I am really professional about my job – even though I really hate getting up in the morning!**"**

## MYLEENE

> **I** We've all got very different personalities, but don't clash. If there's an issue we sit down and discuss it. There hasn't been an argument – yet!**"**

## SUZANNE

> **I** Danny's always positive, always has a smile on his face. He's like my big brother. He's really strong and he has the same insecurities about fame and all that.**"**

## NOEL

# DISCOGRAPHY

### SINGLE

**Pure And Simple /
Bridge Over Troubled Water**

Released March 2001

*Highest chart position: 1*

### ALBUM

**Popstars**

Released March 2001

*Highest chart position: 1*

**Tracks:**

| | |
|---|---|
| Pure And Simple | Carried Away |
| The Way To Your Love | Sweet Alibi |
| One Step Closer | I Didn't Want You Anyway |
| Another Lover | Colour Blind |
| One | Love Will Never End |
| Not The Kind | Monday Monday |
| Make It Happen | Bridge Over Troubled Water |
| Breathe | |

# Welcome

s ang...
conc...
a hook, we are very, very...
the UK. Given the fact that this island we live on is pretty insignificant in the grand scheme of things, it is 'huge' in the world of fly fishing.

It is the history maker, the place where most of the world's fly fishing doyens came from, the birthplace of methods, styles, innovative tackle and patterns taken on board and now used the world over.

This is the country that brought the world the whole concept of dry fly and wet fly/nymph fishing thanks to the writings of both Frederick Halford and George Skues. Halford was so hung up on the whole upstream dry-fly method that he decried any other form of fishing and, in fact, believed that anyone who fished in any other way should not be allowed near running water – the man drew a line in the dirt! This belief still holds true for many anglers today, and on many waters the world over rules dictate that it is the only way to fish!

Thankfully Skues came along with his more adventurous wet/sunk-fly approach and our fishing styles and flies began to develop at a pace and migrated to other parts of the world.

On our lochs and lakes, anglers like W C Stewart, with the advent of new lighter rods, moved away from dapping and fished with teams of wet flies designed to provoke a response from hungry trout: 'loch style' was born, and this too has been taken on the world over. In fact, we Brits have honed this style of fishing and are pretty much world-beaters – everyone else is trying to catch up.

When it comes to aspirational venues and fish species we are very fortunate too, there's so much to go at. We are spoilt for choice: there's river fishing to die for, with trout and grayling from the hallowed chalkstreams, limestone and freestone rivers that we have at our disposal. Our salmon fishing is talked about the world over, and iconic rivers like the mighty Tweed, Tay and Dee hold good numbers of migratory fish. Many anglers aspire to wet a line on these waters, there's so much tradition and history associated with them.

Our stillwater fishing is the envy of many, with great venues, big and small, that are convenient, clean and packed with fish – rainbows, browns, brook, golden and blue trout, you name it, we have it. These intimate venues allow us to further develop many techniques, adapt old ones and create new fly patterns.

More of us are branching out now too, looking to target other species. Predators like pike, zander and perch are high on the list but other coarse fish, like carp, are gaining a huge following; no surprise really – catch a decent sized one on the fly and you'll be hooked too!

Then there's the salt; our little island is surrounded by the sea, which offers even more exciting opportunities. We have only just begun scratching the surface – bass, pollack and mullet are catchable from dry land but we can, if we wish, try for bigger fish from a boat. There are no limits here in the UK.

Yep, we are very lucky indeed, and we hope that this bookazine does a good job of reflecting just some of the amazing fishing on offer out there!

# Contents

# CONTENTS

## FOUR SEASONS IN FLY FISHING

Published by **David Hall Publishing Ltd**. The advertisements and editorial content of this publication are the copyright of **David Hall Publishing Ltd** and may not be quoted, copied or reproduced without prior permission of the publisher. Copyright © 2014

Compiled and edited by **Steve Cullen**
Layout and design by **Nicola Howe**
Sub edited by **David Haynes** and **Victoria Turnbull**
Reprographics by **Derek Mooney** and **Adam Mason**

Spring

The flora and fauna are in full bloom, we're getting our first major hatches and the fish are hungry after the long winter… it's prime time!

# SPRING

# MASTERING MASK

Lyn Davies offers some invaluable advice for fishing Irish loughs during the most unfavourable of weather conditions.

Every May, a friend and I travel over to Ireland to tackle the ever-challenging limestone loughs. My main aim is to catch the mayfly, but you can guarantee, that nine times out of 10 I will be either too early, too late, or it simply isn't a good year for the fly. Countless times, I have heard locals say: "You should have been here last week!" or "The weather is changing next week," when I'd be back home in Swansea! I have learnt to accept that this is fishing, and for visiting anglers there is absolutely nothing we can do about the weather – it will do what it will do.

What's the chance of us visiting anglers catching it right? With this in mind, I have come to realise that you must not get too disappointed when the fishing conditions aren't perfect – they very rarely are and you must simply enjoy the whole experience.

## AS KEEN AS EVER

We arrived in Ballinrobe to stay with my favourite Irish character, Robbie O'Grady. At the age of 72, Robbie, a former world fly fishing champion, is still as keen as ever. Most days you

Mask trout are very colourful and heavily spotted.

will find him on his beloved Lough Mask, either as a ghillie or fishing.

I would recommend, even if you have fished the loughs previously, to have at least one day out with a local boatman. They will show you new water and point out the many hazardous areas that could ruin a day.

Robbie explained that he hadn't been fishing much because the weather had been too warm and bright. Great, the weather was against us again, and it was time for my large hat, shades and huge amounts of sun block. As a visiting angler, you know when the fishing is poor – because that's when the locals aren't out.

## MIGHTY MASK

In my opinion, Carra is the prettiest and safest lough, but the fly come in early May, which we always miss. Corrib is wonderful, as everybody knows, but I fish it a lot every year – time for a change, I wanted to conquer the mighty Mask.

I'd read so much about the place and was determined to gain some confidence fishing it – and the fly were there. I had only fished Mask once previously, and it was a dirty day that even got the locals twitching.

Robbie explained that he had a brand-new boat tied up at Cushlough Bay, with an engine already attached – all we needed was some petrol. It amazes me how much trust the locals have, leaving their boats and engines unlocked during the peak season. You simply couldn't do this in England or Wales – they would be gone. Thankfully, the Irish are generally very trustworthy and, to me, this adds to the whole fishing experience.

Following a trip to the local tackle dealer, the supermarket and petrol station, we were off to Cushlough. Although the weather was far too bright and sunny for an ideal fishing day, mayfly were about and, as ever, if nothing else, we hoped for some spent action later on in the evening. In such bright, calm conditions, it's a perfect opportunity to get to know the lough and, more importantly, get to know it safely. All dangerous rocks are clearly visible and if a fish does move, it can be seen hundreds of yards ahead. In an ideal world, we always like to have an electric motor for stalking fish, especially when spent fishing. Unfortunately, this year, we didn't have access to one – we would have to cope with the oars.

## FOUR PATTERNS FOR MASK

### EPOXY BUZZER

**Hook:** Size 14
**Thread:** Black
**Body:** Black thread or fine floss silk
**Rib:** Fine oval silver tinsel
**Thorax:** Painted orange wing cases over epoxy solution

### GREY WULFF

**Hook:** Size 10
**Thread:** Black
**Wing:** Brown buck tail, tied 'Wulff-style' and divided with the tying thread
**Tail:** Brown buck tail
**Body:** Blue, rabbit underfur
**Hackle:** Blue dun cock and ginger, wound together

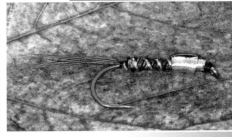

### PEARLY PHEASANT TAIL

**Hook:** Size 12
**Thread:** Black
**Tail, body and wing cases:** Four pheasant tail fibres
**Thorax:** Pearly tinsel
**Rib:** Copper wire

Cushlough is a wonderful bay for the visiting angler. It's easy to find, has an excellent car park and, as a bonus, you've a good chance of meeting local anglers for fishing information. You can experience some excellent, safe fishing just a stone's throw away from the moored boats. It's renowned for its fantastic buzzer hatches because of the ideal depth of water and its weedy bottom – which proves popular for locals at night. I would not like to be motoring around unknown territory in the dark, but when you come into Cushlough you know the area is clear and that you are only a five-minute spin from the car.

We found Robbie's new boat and we set up the rods on the bank. Whenever possible, I would always recommend setting up rods on dry land – it's quicker and easier. If you do it while out on the lough you get yourself into a mess.

### DIFFERENT METHODS

When you are in a boat with another angler on a difficult day, it always pays to initially fish different methods. On this occasion, my friend, Dave, went deeper, with an intermediate and some small wets, while I opted for a dry fly.

You need to cover all options until you discover fish, so always keep a close eye out for rising fish and watch out for congregating boats. They are probably there for a good reason and again, talk to as many anglers as possible.

My dry-fly set up was a bit different. Robbie had explained that a local angler had done well at a competition using what he called, 'The Hanging Epoxy' a method similar to the 'washing line' technique. You simply fish a dry fly on the top dropper and a team of small epoxy buzzers or nymphs below. I liked the sound of this set-up.

I had a visible sight bob with the dry fly (a small Green Wulff), which could always attract a stray fish, but I was also fishing a few feet under.

### WATCH THE BIRDIES

Always keep an eye on the water for hatching fly and take note of what's going on in the air. The gulls are a welcome sight. If you see them working a bay – get over there, you can guarantee there are fly hatching. Where there is fly, in time, there will be fish.

It is tempting on such a large water to motor off towards the horizon to do large drifts.

This is fine, in ideal conditions, but when times are hard you need to be on the move as much as possible and searching out where the deep water meets shallow, along the shore lines. It's hard work, because with small drifts you are constantly positioning the boat – but this is how the locals do it.

You rarely see a local fishing over deep, uninteresting water during this time of year. So learn from the masters and work the shorelines. If nothing else, you'll hit into a few smaller fish to raise your confidence levels. Remember, a boat can drift quickly, even in the lightest of winds, and the most reliable of engines can let you down. Always start the engine in plenty of time to get off the shore safely. The man on the engine has a responsible job with this type of fishing, while the other lucky angler can fish out the drift to the bitter end.

### SPENT FLY

We fished hard for many hours, only to pick off a few small fish close to the water's edge. The odd mayfly was hatching, but there wasn't the amount of fly about to bring on the fish. You must remember, these fish are wild and have a phenomenal amount of food at their disposal. They will not go out of their way to take a struggling mayfly on the surface, when they are probably already stuffed full of nymphs and other deeper-living creatures.

We noticed a fair amount of spent congregating in one of the bays, so we decided to hang around and continue to work the area

When the light starts to go, the 'spent' fly will fall on the water.

## SPENT MAYFLY

**Hook:** Size 12

**Thread:** Black

**Body and tail:** Detachable see-through plastic tube, with a large white cock hackle pulled through the centre. Create the black tail fibres and 'barred' segmented-body effect by painting lines on the hackle with a black, waterproof marker pen beforehand.

**Hackle:** Large black cock hackle, tied down with a figure of eight to imitate the mayfly's wings, spent on the water.

**Note:** Being such a specialised tying (and for the amount of time you will actually use one), I would recommend purchasing them from local tackle dealers. Try and find the lightly dressed variations.

## TOP TIPS:

• Fish with the most streamlined of buzzers over weedy areas.

• Have a day afloat with a local boatman.

• Always keep your dry flies well greased.

in hope of some trout latching onto them. Drift after drift I cast out my team and just kept in contact with the dry fly on the top, in case a fish showed an interest. Dry-fly fishing can be hard work, especially when you are constantly watching a small fly in a wave, but it's usually worth the effort in the end, so I am always confident to sit through quiet periods.

We were approaching the end of a drift, when I felt a solid take a few feet under, not far from the rushes that lined the approaching bank. I was into a nice fish of about 1½lb – and it had taken one of my nymphs. After a great little fight, the fish was safely in the net and available for inspection. It was a beautiful brown trout, sporting huge black spots and a spade-like tail – so typical of Mask fish. I had done it, I had outwitted a wild fish with a tiny Pheasant Tail on the point – and it was my own dressing!

Confidence levels were high; I had proved to myself that I could catch a fish in difficult conditions and – where there is one, there should be more. Sadly, this was not the case and I fished on without a touch.

We began to see the odd fish rising in the bay, although they looked small, they were feeding fish, so we decided to get on top of them. As hoped, they were scooping up the previously seen flies trapped in the surface. Dave decided to change to a floater and try his luck with a single spent-mayfly pattern.

## KEEP IT SIMPLE

I am a firm believer that when spent-gnat fishing, it is better to keep things simple and use a short leader and single fly. If it happens, action is hectic and brief, so you need to be able to cast in the path of a cruising fish with the minimum of fuss. I kept to the same set-up. I had a dry on the top, so I felt confident enough that if I cast to a rising fish, it would take a look at the fly.

By this time, like a flick of a switch, the wind had changed direction and the rises had stopped. The fish had gone down – it was over. We were lucky to be in the right place, at the right time. Was it luck, or did we reap the reward of being observant anglers? I'd like to think it was a bit of both. It goes to show, you should always be ready for a quick change and make the most of your opportunities – they are few and far between in such difficult conditions.

There were no other boats around us, but that's the beauty of these loughs – depending on the wind direction, water depth and fly hatches – every bay offers a new experience.

We fished until the sun set, but the breeze was cold. It was one of those evenings when something is telling you that you'd be better off sitting in a pub with a pint of the black stuff – we reeled in and headed for shore. I was content that we had caught a couple of nice fish in such difficult conditions.

## LOUGH MASK FACT FILE

**Location:** West coast of Ireland, near Ballinrobe
**Size:** 22,000 acres

In the net! Despite the occasional mayfly on the water, the PTN scores well.

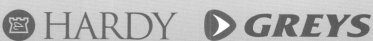

# A TASTE OF THE
# TWEED

Scottish international and stillwater master Dave
Downie samples the Borders' finest as he takes on
a new-found challenge – river fishing.

Being predominantly a stillwater
competition angler for many
years, I was beginning to search
for a change – in the form of
rivers. This was mainly due to
the challenge of learning new skills, but
also the increased 'comfort level', whereby I
could not only go fishing but really enjoy my
surroundings and, at times, just sit back and
enjoy the peace and tranquillity that flowing
water brings.

So it was with much excitement that I
was up early after a night of Guinness and
fishing conversations with Total FlyFisher's
friends. With breakfast eaten it was off to the
St Boswells AC stretch of the mighty River
Tweed. The gun shop was the first stop, where
we bought our permits and stocked up on
any essentials that would be required for our
angling adventure. Upon arrival at the shop
we met up with a good friend of mine from
Galashiels, Steve Cullen. Steve has been fishing
the Tweed and surrounding rivers for five or
six years now and has caught grayling to over
4lb and trout in excess of 5lb. He was going to
be our guide for the day, as I am still a relative
beginner and need all the help I can get!

Tickets were purchased and it was time to
head to Mertoun Bridge, which would be our
base of operations for the day.

Our 9am arrival was a wee bit early for the
Tweed trout if we were hoping to catch them
on the dries, as Steve explained to us that the
rise would not normally get into full swing until
11am. I set up my 9ft 6-wt Bloke rod, which at
first may seem a little overgunned. However,
the Tweed is a big river and you will often need
to throw a long line into the seemingly ever-
present breeze. Also, large browns inhabit the
river – you never quite know what you are
going to hook.

I tied up a tapered leader consisting of
Sightfree G3 with a 3ft, 10lb butt, followed
by three feet of 8lb, three feet of 6lb and, at
the end, two feet of 4lb. With a size 12 Olive
Klinkhamer tied on and tippet degreased, I was
ready to go.

## MICRO-DRAG

On the way down to the river, Steve was told
us the ins and outs, explaining to us that small
discrepancies in the current could cause 'micro-
drag'. This entails the fly skating – even if only
for an inch or so – and will look unnatural
and put the fish down. Perfect presentation is
therefore the key to catching.

Nearly there! Dave's
two-pounder finally
comes to the net
after a terrific battle.

# Spring

With talk of a fish of nearly 5lb taken on the dry fly off the Melrose stretch a few days prior by river keeper Tam McLeish, I could not wait to get fishing, in the hope that I could just catch one decent fish!

On walking down the riverbank, olives were hatching sporadically, with a couple of fish feeding readily below the Mertoun Bridge. Steve spotted a few fish moving on the far bank of the pool and headed out into the river to have a few exploratory casts. It was a pleasure to watch Steve wading carefully, popping his Olive Emerger accurately above the trout while all the time mending the line to iron out even the slightest hint of drag. Eventually a fish was fooled, coming up for Steve's pattern at pace – a little too quick for Steve! Much to his dismay – and with a few well-chosen words, which cannot be printed – he moved onto the next steadily rising fish.

## MIDDLE MERTOUN

I suggested we move to the middle section I had fished the previous week with Scottish National Rivers Champion Jake Harvey, who showed me a thing or two, taking trout to around the 2lb mark. So, off we went down the river to the Middle Mertoun beat, which, incidentally, sits in Jake's back garden – some people have all the luck!

To reach Middle Mertoun you can either cross the river and go down the left-hand bank – depending on water height – or take the steep path through the woods, which runs alongside the river and gives you a good bird's-eye view of the trout. We stopped at several viewing points to watch many small fish moving consistently under the trees, with the odd bigger trout sliding out of the deeper water to intercept olive duns on the surface. In my short river career I've found that time taken to observe the fish feeding is always time well spent – it gives clues to the flies they are taking, how fast they are moving to take them and even how picky they are likely to be!

## RISING FISH

On arriving at Middle Mertoun, we were greeted by rising fish from the off, and in the same areas where I had seen them the week before. Steve pointed out that some of the better fish we could see moving were large Tweed grayling. Mertoun holds some true jumbos and fish in excess of 2lb are very common indeed, especially when fishing heavy bugs in the winter months.

I moved upstream and into a position that I could cast my dry in front of one of the fish and hopefully not spook him by causing drag. I tried a few different dries, had several missed chances, and landed some smaller fish but not

Steve Cullen picks up a small brown from a seam near the far bank.

## THREE FOR THE TWEED

### OLIVE CDC EMERGER
**Hook:** Kamasan B100, sizes 12 to 16
**Thread:** Light cahill
**Body:** Light cahill thread
**Rib:** Light olive Flexi-Floss
**Wing:** Natural CDC
**Hackle:** Red game cock, clipped underneath

### OLIVE ANTRON UPRIGHT
**Hook:** Kamasan B400, sizes 12 to 16
**Thread:** Light cahill
**Tail:** Antron strands
**Body:** Light olive rabbit
**Wing:** Grey Antron
**Hackle:** Light dun cock

Careful wading means that you can get close to rising fish, perfect for dry-fly fishing.

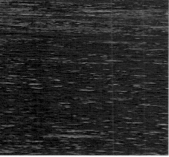

## SC OLIVE NYMPH

**Hook:** Kamasan B400, sizes 12 to 16
**Thread:** Light cahill, black for head
**Underbody:** Fine lead wire
**Body:** Light cahill thread
**Rib:** Light olive Flexi-Floss
**Tail:** Red game cock
**Thorax:** Hare's ear dubbing
**Thorax cover:** Brown Body Stretch

the one I was after. Reverting to the same Olive Klinkhamer that I had used the previous week, a couple of casts later, my rod was bending and buckling under the strain of a grayling of around 1lb. After Steve quickly caught some fish at the tail of the pool – with a few decent ones among them – we headed back up towards the pool below the bridge to see if the rise had begun in earnest.

It turned out to be the rule of the day unfortunately, as the strong, chilly breeze did nothing to encourage more olives to hatch. They simply came off the water in dribs and drabs and, as such, the trout only fed sporadically. A few fish were moving in the slower water beyond a fast seam below Mertoun Bridge and I for one found it difficult getting my Klinkhamer to fish naturally in the conflicting currents. A couple of small fish later, and with the temptation of a broad-shouldered brown moving close to the far bank, I reached for my wading staff. Especially during higher water, this is a must on the Tweed – helping you keep upright over slippery stones as well as determining the depth of the water you are just about to step into.

### KLINKHAMER SUCCESS

Up came the fish again. The line flew out perfectly and the fly – finally – drifted downstream, settled neatly on the surface film. This was the cast. As if by clockwork, up he came and wolfed the fly down. A quick strike,

the surface churned and the trout was not at all amused. Jump after jump my heart pounded as I tried to bully the 1lb-plus brown away from the strong current – I can only imagine what a three-pounder would be like!

Finally coming to the net, the full-spotted trout waited patiently to have its picture taken before returning to the peat-stained water – that's what we came here for!

### DEEP WADING

Sitting back with a 'pleased as punch' smile, I did not think the day could get any better. Yet, another good fish came up in an even more challenging position, right across the river, and started rising confidently to the few olives being carried on the current. A deeper wade was required, coupled with a tricky cast to pitch the fly beyond a fast seam into the slower

Steve's fly box reveals the characteristically chunky dries favoured on the Tweed.

A beautifully marked wild brown goes back to the peaty crystal-clear water of the River Tweed.

water where the fish was lying. After making five or six casts downstream of the fish, to judge the distance, the first proper cast went out. I watched the fly closely as the trout simply lifted in the water, taking the fly so gently it would be easy to have missed it. As I did! Recasting immediately, the brown took much harder this time and there was no mistaking the strike. As if tethered to a tow truck, the 6-wt hooped over under the full force of the fish. Five minutes of pure panic later and my biggest dry-caught trout from any river lay in the bottom of the net. At a little over 2lb it wasn't anything unusual for the river but, to me, wild fishing surely cannot get any better.

## A BREATH OF FRESH AIR

Coming from a mainly stillwater upbringing, fishing for wild and stocked browns on my local Gryffe Reservoir in Port Glasgow and Loch Leven, I found it a breath of fresh air to fish on running water. Everything is different, the tackle, the surroundings and, most of all, the attitude of river anglers. The general atmosphere is one of friendliness but with a little good-humoured competitiveness thrown in the mix. I found I had to adapt to using lighter tippets, different-style dries and having to stop and think about everything before casting a fly to a rising trout. Even if you managed to drop your dry in the right place,

would it need mending upstream, downstream or what? How do you get rid of that drag that all the seams in the river are trying so hard to put into your fly? These are all things that I look forward to learning in the future through practice. It gives a great sense of achievement when that fish comes up and takes a dry you have tied, with confidence.

Fishing the River Tweed is not easy at the best of times and it pays to just watch the river to get to know it in all its states. When it is low it will show up all those holes and rocks and general fish-holding pots and pits. Local knowledge is such a big help and I have been lucky that many good angling friends of mine come from the Tweed, and have given me a head start. The true Tweed monsters may have eluded us on the day, but as a dodgy actor once said – I'll be back.

CONTACTS
Borders Gun Room,
St Boswells
Tel: 01835 822844
Web: www.bordersgunroom.co.uk

Now we're talking... over 2lb of stunning, dry-fly-caught Mertoun gold.

# GAME ANGLING
## C O N S U L T A N C Y
- *UK'S LARGEST GAME FISHING RETAILER* -

# RIVER FISHING
## SPECIALISTS

t selection of lines, flies & hooks

er 200+ rods & reels

WE HAVE OFFERS ON ROD & REEL COMBOS

We have everything for the river angler, with a massive selection of rods, reels, lines, flies, fly-tying equipment, wire, hooks, waders & clothing.

Unit 22, Robinsons Industrial Est, Shaftesbury St, Derby, DE23 8NL
Tel: 01332 331548 // www.gameanglingconsultancy.com

Follow us on

Fly-tying maestro George Barron takes a closer look at traditional fly styles, and highlights some of his favourites. To start, winged wets!

# FAMILY VALUES

When I pack the vice and hit the road to demonstrate traditional fly-tying techniques at the numerous shows around the UK and Ireland, and around the very popular Fly Dressers Guild circuit, most of the problem-solving questions that I'm continually asked relate to winged wet flies.

Questions as simple as: "What feathers do I use and why?" "How do you stop them splitting when tying in?" and "Does the addition of a wing make any difference to the effectiveness of the wet fly?"

I'll deal with the various winging feathers I use first and why I often prefer them to the authentic age-old feathers suggested in the original dressings.

I wouldn't consider some old traditional winging feathers, such as tawny owl, bittern and nightjar, nowadays, simply from the point of view of preservation of the species, and because there are plenty of alternatives easier acquired.

Matching slips from wing quills and possibly tail feathers – teal flank and bronze mallard excepted – will, to my mind, just about cover all wet-fly winging requirements.

A list comprising hen pheasant secondary quills and tails, jay wings, various duck wings such as mallard and mandarin, and at a push starling for smaller fly sizes, and you're just about covered; chuck in magpie tails if black or dark wings are required.

Hen pheasant secondary feathers dyed in soft golden olive, light claret and maybe grey colours give more variations on the theme. I like to get my hen pheasant secondary quills from young hen birds because I think they're softer and more 'webby'. To get them, I help out at a syndicated pheasant shoot during the close season, a situation that provides me with the pick of the feathers I require, not just for winging but also quality tails from cock birds.

I do think wings on wet flies make a difference to the effectiveness of the fly, certainly if they are tied in before the head hackle, contrary to many dressings that show the wing tied in last. The reason being, in my humble opinion and because it works for me I suppose, is they support the hackle and stop it collapsing around the body, and to my mind that creates far more lifelike movement in the finished fly.

## PROFILE

George Barron has been a regular in the Welsh international team since gaining his first cap in 1986, is a team member of highly successful Llanilar AA, and has been heavily involved in the competition scene for over 30 years. He has run the popular Ty Nant Classic invitational competition since 1998 and demonstrates traditional fly tying at all the major shows.

George's preference is to fish and tie flies for the wild trout waters in the UK and Ireland.

Putting the wing on before the head hackle is one of the few areas in traditional wet-fly tying where I differ in opinion from the views expressed by others on the subject, certainly in the tying of wet olive patterns where a highly defined black or dark-centred hackle, such as greenwell or badger, dyed or natural, creates a more realistic olive effect.

Length of head hackle is also important. As a template, I like to dress my olive wet flies with the hackle reaching along the body, about the same length as the wing. This is done easily enough.

To tie in matching quill slips without splitting the fibres is quite simple. Firstly, build up a bed using tying thread to set the wings on, roughly level with the body. Keeping the thread tight to the body end, offer the wing onto the bed, held tight between thumb and forefinger.

Take the first turn of thread in between your fingers and lightly down over the wing but don't pull tight, then take a second turn of thread over the wing and pull it tight. Add a few more firm wraps moving forward before removing your grip on the wing and it should be set nicely in place. The wing will only split if you bring the thread back beyond the first wrap you put on – simple.

Let's have a look at what are the most popular winged wet flies around – the time of season, type of hatch we're imitating and, obviously, the venue being the deciding factors prior to choice. Personal favourites usually get tied on before other offerings because they've likely produced the goods in the past and most of us feel more confident using tried-and-tested banker flies.

I'm going to list six of the winged wet flies that have got me in among the fish over the years; most of them are fairly universal and travel well, some are traditional and some have slight variations on standard, conventional dressings.

## THE COCH-YN-LAS (red and blue)

Shooting back across the Irish Sea, here's another very old fly pattern that I jazzed up a few years ago. It's done okay for me on the Welsh mountain lakes and still gets a swim if I'm walking the bank chasing 9in brownies when the Coch beetle is hatching.

Funny thing about Welsh wet flies, most of them don't have tails but lots of them have wings.

This is basically a conventional Coch with a couple of updates and a wing, but it's caught me many wild trout when fished on the top dropper with a recognised wet Coch pattern on the dropper below.

**Hook:** Wet fly, sizes 10 and 12
**Rib:** Copper wire
**Body:** Strands of peacock herl
**First hackle:** Magenta hen
**Wing:** Blae duck or jay
**Head hackle:** Dark centred, Greenwell hen

## PIN FRY INVICTA VARIATION

I think that most anglers associate wet flies of any description as originating predominately from the three Celtic countries and possibly creeping in from the north of England. While the Celts still fished with pulled wet flies to put food on the table, the Anglo-Saxon crowd down the other end of the UK preferred a more leisurely approach when confronted with catching trout on the slow-running streams and stillwaters in the soft south.

Bushy dry flies that sat dead on the surface or nymph imitations that lay comatose below the surface seemed to do the job, albeit there was very little life in these offerings to stir a trout.

However, I do believe the Silver Invicta to be one of the few winged wet flies with its roots firmly planted in England.

I like the conventional hackled pattern for sedges and my own body-free hackled version when the trout move onto pin fry about a half to one inch long.

Cast into the disturbance of feeding fish and just allow to drop through the water; if no response after a few seconds, one long pull and stop seems to work. Tie this pattern in a size 14 and dispense with the JC cheeks and it's a great corixa pattern.

**Hook:** Wet fly, sizes 10 and 12
**Tail:** Yellow toppings
**Body:** Silver tinsel
**Rib:** Fine silver wire
**Wing:** Hen pheasant secondary
**Head hackle:** Two or three turns light red game
**Cheeks:** JC splits, blue jay throat hackle (optional)

## SOOTY OLIVE

This is surely one of the most utilitarian fly patterns in history, equally effective in any corner of the UK and Ireland.

It carries the usual baggage of having many slightly bastardised variations falling under the umbrella of the 'Sooty' brand name, mostly changes relevant to the body or hackle colour. The dressing I utilise on most of my trips to Ireland nowadays is a fair bit different from the original in more ways than one.

I think it was one of Mike Noone's successful olive patterns early season on Corrib but it travels well. Brian Leadbetter once told me a favourite Rutland fly of his was the Sooty Olive when the fish were just sub-surface; what better endorsement for a winged wet fly? This fishes anywhere on the cast and on most lines depending on the weather. Some versions favour a wing of folded bronze mallard, but I'm not a great believer in that material in this instance, although I do use it on other lighter olive patterns. For me it's matching slips of blae duck quill or jay.

**Hook:** Wet fly, sizes 12 and 14
**Tail:** Dyed sunburst, tippets
**Rib:** UTC wire, small red
**Body:** Sooty olive seal's fur, brushed out
**Wing:** Blae duck quills
**Head hackle:** Hen, dyed sooty
**Cheeks:** JC splits

## MURT FOLAN'S RAYMOND VARIANT

One of the nice things when writing about flies, given an unrestricted copy remit by the editor (bit of a soft touch), is that it gives you the chance to resurrect patterns that have slipped out of favour for no particular reason. They provide a nice aside from the normal dose of Dabbler rehashes that seem to clog the fishing press conveyor belt.

An old Irish pattern I love using, especially on Melvin and Mask, is my take on Murt Folan's Raymond. A fishing legend in Ireland, I haven't seen Murt for a few years but I hear he's well – his son Colin is fisheries manager on Lough Inagh.

Anyway, nothing really special about the wing on this fly, it's there to simply complement the rest of a very busy and colourful dressing.

This fly is an exercise in what traditional fly tying is all about. Enjoy.

**Hook:** Wet fly, sizes 10 and 12
**Tail:** Natural toppings
**Rib:** UTC wire, hot yellow
**Body:** Yellow seal's fur
**Body hackle:** Crimson hen, I often use orange
**Wing:** Hen pheasant secondary
**Head hackles:** Grizzle hen dyed blue and golden olive hen, tied together

## GREEN PETER

While we're in Ireland, let's run with a similar standard winged wet fly.

The Peter, as it's affectionately known, also has so many plays on the original dressing you could write a feature on it alone. An all-season-round pattern, equally effective in a sedge or mayfly hatch and almost a first pick on the cast if it's salmon you're after. Normally tied on a size 10 or even bigger in Ireland, it's a real scratch-the-surface weapon but, strangely, I've always done best with it in a size 12.

At times the trout like this on Brenig, especially up the arm of the same name when the sedges come off. I prefer a light hen pheasant secondary wing to the conventional hen pheasant tail.

**Hook:** Wet fly, sizes 10 and 12
**Butt:** Smidgen of red seal's fur, or red holo
**Rib:** UTC wire, hot yellow, small
**Body:** Apple green seal's fur
**Body hackle:** Palmered red game or rusty dun hen
**Wing:** Hen pheasant secondary, or same dyed light golden olive
**Head hackle:** Longish, red game/rusty dun

## MALLARD AND CLARET

Like the Greenwell's Glory and the Bibio, the Mallard And Claret has a solid, traditional history. It is possibly one of the most commonly referred to wet flies around.

Good flies aren't spectacular, they're basic and do the job – they catch fish.

Tie it on anywhere on the cast, anywhere in the country, any river or stillwater, and I'll bet you a pound to a penny it'll get you a trout. The modern aficionados of fly fishing – the Blob and Booby men – likely don't even have one in their fly boxes, but come a hard competition day and the old M&C could prove their salvation.

Once again the traditional dressing suggested a bronze mallard wing. I tie mine with either a blae duck quill or, as always, hen pheasant secondary in its many guises.

It's nothing to do with winging I know, but when tying olive patterns kick the conventional four turns of rib into touch. Natural olive bodies are very heavily segmented so, when ribbing, incorporate about six or even eight tight turns of wire through the body. It's much closer to the real thing.

**Hook:** Wet fly, sizes 10 and 12
**Tail:** Natural tippets
**Rib:** UTC wire hot yellow
**Body:** Dark claret seal's fur
**Wing:** Blae duck or hen pheasant secondary
**Hackle:** Well-marked natural or dyed greenwell

Due to a harsh environment, waterborne fly life can be scarce on many upland reservoirs. However, when terrestrials are blown onto the water it's party time for trout.

# THE ALTERNATIVE MAYFLY

The hawthorn fly is a strange insect. Appearing for only a couple of weeks at a time, often in droves, it comes across as the clown of the six-legged world. Witness a horde of hawthorns trying to navigate on a windy day and you'll see why - they were at the back of the queue when flying skills were handed out. Furthermore, take this land-borne insect and add water and the poor little blighters don't stand a chance. Good news for the fish.

Contrary to popular belief, hatches of hawthorns are not restricted to moorland; that is acidic environments. The Midlands'

reservoirs, many small stillwaters and even chalkstreams, experience hatches each year; it's just that for a real 'hawthorn madness' session, windswept upland lakes are usually the first port of call.

Yes, 'hawthorn madness'. It really can be that frantic. Like the lucky anglers who get to experience fishing a true mayfly hatch, hawthorn time is the peak of the season on many waters. One such venue is Stithians Lake in mid-Cornwall.

A barren and often bleak water, this 270-acre lake is home to one of the biggest hawthorn hatches in Britain and Ireland.

Don't wade too deep — you can expect to find feeding fish in surprisingly shallow water.

# Spring

## HAWTHORN

This is a 'proper' hawthorn pattern. More realistic imitations can be an advantage during periods of calm or bright weather. If angling pressure has been high, fishing during the last few days of the hawthorn period can become tricky. Therefore for 'wise' trout, give this one a chuck.

**Hook:** Down-eyed dry fly, sizes 10 to 14
**Body:** Fine black dubbing
**Wings:** Two white hackle tips
**Legs:** Knotted black hackle stalks
**Hackle:** Black cock

## THE EX-HOPPER

The Ex-Hopper is so-called because the pattern came about after a standard Black Hopper fell apart. The scruffiness gives the fly that essential image of confusion on the water's surface – if you were to pick one fly for hawthorn fishing, make it this one.

**Hook:** Medium-shanked, down-eyed dry fly, sizes 8 to 12
**Body:** Black seal's fur tied as scruffily as possible!
**Hackle:** Black cock

At times during the first two weeks of May, the clouds of the insect are so prolific that it's like a scene from Hitchcock's The Birds; although, admittedly in miniature and with less squawking. The bumbling insects are everywhere, colliding with each other, vegetation, even anglers and, nine times out of 10, end up in the water. Give a few days from the start of 'hawthorn season' for the trout to switch on and you'll find yourself in the middle of a merciless feeding frenzy and, as a result, some of the finest dry-fly fishing you'll ever encounter.

### TACKLE TIPS

There's no point in dressing up the fishing methods, describing fancy leaders, close-copy patterns or 'essential' complex casts. This is simple, 'action all the way' fishing and it's bloody good fun. During the peak of the hawthorn period, the trout couldn't care less about how good your fly looks on the water. The fish are looking up for something black and straggly and if your fly is black and straggly and floats to some degree they'll eat it.

The only apparent reason for a feeding fish refusing an artificial hawthorn is if the leader is visible, floating on the surface. This rings true for 90 per cent of dry-fly fishing, so the number-one tip for presentation is to degrease – that is, sink – that leader.

Your standard stillwater rod will do the job – perhaps a 6-wt or 7-wt. On calmer or brighter days, when delicate presentation is an advantage, try a 5-wt if you've got one. It's also more fun when you hook that overwintered three-pounder and realise you can't stop it.

Talking of overwintered fish. On many

> "As with all imitative fishing, present your artificial in the same manner as the natural insects would act."

It's a good idea to have your net on you; attached to a D ring on your back is ideal…

TIP

When fishing in heavy ripple, fly floatant will keep your fly buoyant for that little bit longer. You don't want it to float like a cork though!

… and it's then just a case of grabbing it when you need it!

waters, hawthorn time is when those elusive giants that you 'always knew were in there somewhere' come out to play. Those fish that for the remainder of the season will be lurking among the boulders, stalking sticklebacks and the like, simply cannot turn down such a feast and therefore it's often your best chance of connecting with one. Unless you see a monster bulging on the surface, yes, it may be a case of fishing in a lucky dip. You'll just have to plough your way through all those one-and-half-pounders until you strike it lucky. It's a hard life.

## EXCESS WIND CAN BE GOOD

Taking into account the hawthorn's lack of aviation talent, the angler's greatest ally is the wind. Banks where even a gentle breeze blows onto the water will be a good starting point. Where these banks are covered in long, moorland grasses, gorse and alders, all the better. Hawthorns will cling to these features en masse, so when a sudden gust knocks them to the surface of the water, it's not long before a trail of the drowning bugs is gradually swept out into the lake. The trout are never far away.

As with all imitative fishing, present your artificial in the same manner as the natural insect.

In this case the fly should drift with the wind, twitching and struggling every so often before eventually going under. A trick that will often pick up a bonus fish is to retrieve the fly slowly once it has sunk. The fact that fish will

## MUDDLER HOPPER

For days when strong winds blow and the water becomes choppy, a deer-hair head helps keep the fly in the surface film. The red colour enables you to spot it in the wave and doesn't seem to make any difference to the fish. The wake caused by occasionally twitching the pattern will draw trout from all corners!

**Hook:** Wet fly, sizes 10 to 14
**Head:** Red deer hair
**Body:** Black and red seal's fur, mixed
**Rib:** Flat pearl tinsel
**Legs:** Knotted black pheasant tail fibres
**Hackle:** Black cock

After a right royal runaround, Richard lands more than 3lb of pristine Stithians' rainbow trout.

take hawthorns readily sub-surface also hints to the way they take the flies off the top – by drowning them first.

When trout take large insects, it's common to see them 'slash' or crash at the surface. Upon lifting the rod, the angler is often left standing somewhat bemused, as the fly is left untouched and the fish is long gone. Unfortunately this situation is all too common when fishing hawthorns

and the reason is simple. The fish will roll on the insect (or your artificial for that matter) to sink it. The prey is therefore rendered totally vulnerable and the fish can take its time to turn and swallow the fly as it sinks.

If you experience this frustration when striking at 'rising' fish, there is a solution. Resist the temptation to strike. Let the fish boil, roll or slash at the fly and gently take up any slack line on the water's surface. What – fingers crossed – usually follows is a sharp pull as said fish turns to casually take the sinking fly. Lift your rod now – and you're in!

Hawthorn season provides the cream of the year's sport at many moorland reservoirs. Stithians' regular Richard Buckingham shows the quality of fish to expect.

## TEN TOP TIPS

1 Overcast, breezy days are best.

2 Fish from banks where the wind is blowing onto the water.

3 Banks with gorse, grasses, scrub and trees will hold most hawthorn flies.

4 Hawthorns are usually at their most prolific from midday onwards.

5 Keep on the move if the action slows up.

6 Degrease your leader every dozen or so casts.

7 The scruffier the fly, the better.

8 Don't strike immediately – wait for a pull.

9 Don't always wait to see fish rise – they could be taking the drowned hawthorns.

10 Never put a light bulb in your back pocket.

# COCH-Y-BONDDU BOOKS

Machynlleth, Mid-Wales SY20 8DG    Tel: 01654 702837    www.anglebooks.com    orders@anglebooks.com

**FLYTYER'S MASTERCLASS**
Slightly bumped. £30.00  £9.95

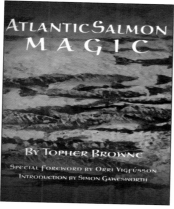

**ATLANTIC SALMON MAGIC**
Hbk  £100.00  £50.00

**CASTING WITH LEFTY KREH**
Hbk    £30.00    £9.95

**FLYFISHER'S HANDBOOK**
Hbk    £25.00   £14.95

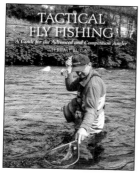

**TACTICAL FLY FISHING**
Hbk  £25.00  £9.95

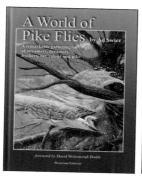

**A WORLD OF PIKE
FLIES Hbk  £25.00**

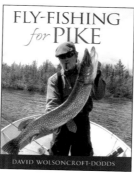

**FLY-FISHING FOR PIKE**
Hbk    £25.00    £9.95

**IRISH MAYFLIES**
Hbk   £25.00

**FLY FISHING OUTSIDE
THE BOX  Hbk  £25.00**

**SALMON FLIES**
Pbk  £19.95

**BROOK & RIVER
TROUTING Pbk  £19.95**

**NORTH COUNTRY FLIES**
Pbk   £19.95

**THE PRACTICAL ANGLER**
Pbk   £19.95

**TYING FLIES IN THE
IRISH STYLE Hbk  £25.00**

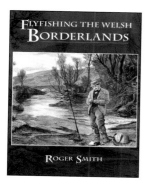

**WELSH BORDERLANDS**
Pbk £25.00

**ROGER WOOLLEY**
Pbk  £25.00

**WET-FLY TYING & FISHING**
Hbk   £25.00  £9.95

**RIVER TROUT FLIES**
Pbk  £14.95  £7.95

**FLIES OF DERBYS & STAFFS**
Hbk   £35.00  £9.95

*10,000 different angling books, old & new, are in stock & on our website - www.anglebooks.com*
*Mastercard / Visa / Maestro / Paypal*    POSTAGE EXTRA UP TO A MAXIMUM OF £5    *Overseas postage at cost*

# WATERHEN BLOA

This is a very simple fly that has accounted for so many trout and grayling over the years, and will no doubt continue to do so for years to come!

**Hook:** Kamasan B175, size 14
**Thread:** Pearsall's Gold
**Dubbing:** Natural mole
**Hackle:** Waterhen

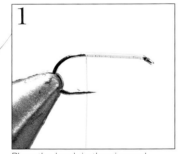

**1**

Place the hook in the vice and, using touching turns, create a bed of thread, stopping just behind the hook point.

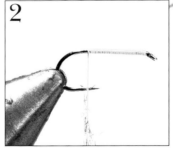

**2**

Now take a small amount of the mole fur and create a thin and wispy dubbing rope.

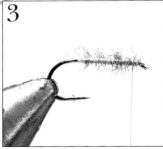

**3**

Wind up the body in touching turns, stopping a little behind the eye.

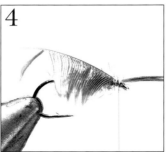

**4**

Strip one side of the waterhen hackle and catch in behind the eye by the tips.

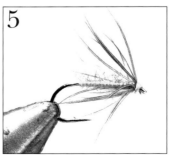

**5**

Wind the hackle around the shank twice and secure with tying thread. Whip finish and trim.

**6**

Add a drop of varnish, making sure none goes on the feather. If any gets in the eye pull a hackle stalk through to clean.

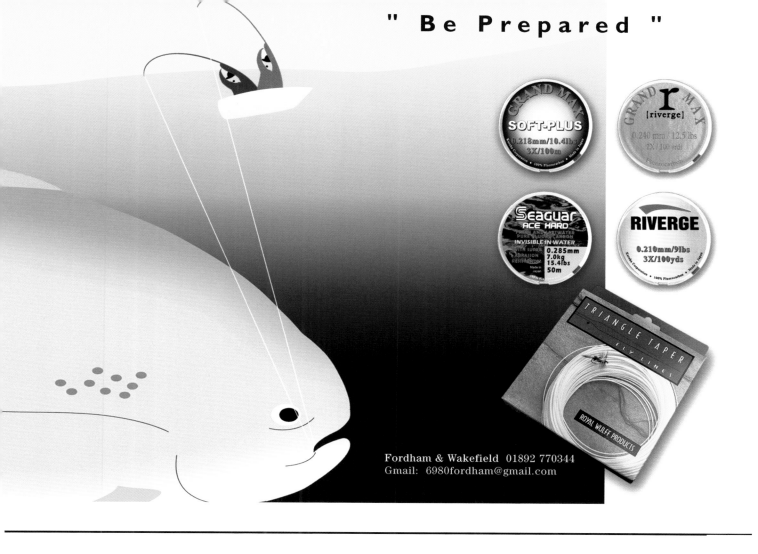

# SUMMER

We spend more time on the water during summer, and no wonder – good weather, good company and great fishing!

Scottish reservoir ace Jim Crawford takes to the Midlands' mighty Rutland Water to explain all you need to know about tackling buzzer hatches with dries…

# DRIFTING ON GIANT WATERS

Dry-fly fishing is probably the most visually exciting and enthralling part of our sport. It also demands a certain degree of skill to cast to locate the fish, to match the hatch and then to present your fly in a natural manner. These skills are as important today as they have been for more than 100 years!

Most of our early dry-fly fishing will be based around midge patterns, whether it be flies that are fished on the surface or actually IN the surface film. For example, shuttlecock patterns, where the cul-de-canard (CDC) feathers are tied forward of the eye of the hook, allow the body of the fly to be suspended below the surface of the water, matching flies that are just about to hatch.

To represent the fully hatched adult insects that sit ON the surface, we may choose a Sedge Hog, parachute or stimulator style pattern.

To be honest, it is hard to categorise some flies because the modern-day dries are so versatile and can be made to represent different stages of an insect's life cyle simply by applying floatant to a particular area of the fly.

For this feature I was lucky enough to spend a day on Rutland Water with my mate Stuart Hume.

# Summer

## JIM'S TOP RESERVOIR DRIES

### HALF HOG
**Hook:** Fulling Mill dry fly, size 12
**Thread:** Olive 8/0
**Body:** Olive micro UV Straggle
**Wing:** Olive buck deer hair
**Legs:** Olive pheasant tail fibres, knotted
**Note:** Colours can be altered to suit hatch

### WAEF MIDGE
**Hook:** Fulling Mill dry fly, size 12
**Thread:** Black 8/0
**Tail:** Twisted black Flexi Floss
**Body:** Black micro UV Straggle
**Wing:** Natural CDC
**Hackle:** Black cock, clipped underneath

### SHUTTLECOCK
**Hook:** Kamasan B400
**Body:** Lureflash Multi-Colour
**Thorax:** Red micro UV Straggle
**Wing:** Six CDC feathers, clipped

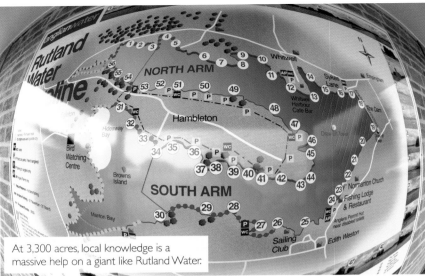

At 3,300 acres, local knowledge is a massive help on a giant like Rutland Water.

Large, overwintered rainbows are the targets for the dry-fly fisher.

Two days prior to my visit I received a text on my mobile from Iain Barr; he was out on Rutland filling his boots with 3lb-plus rainbows on dries!

It turned out that he had been drifting on open water all the way along the Manton Shore across to Yellowstone... the place was alive.

They were feeding hard on large black midges, which is something I have witnessed in the past but never on the scale that I was to witness that weekend – it was amazing.

With fish feeding on both drowned flies and those skittering across the surface that weekend, I had the best dry-fly fishing I have ever experienced.

I watched with great interest the large browns coming up and slapping the emerging flies with their tails to drown them! In fact, when targeting the fish in that area, Stuart and I both hooked browns slightly above the tail. Those fish were so fast; sometimes your line would tighten and you would catch the slightest glimpse of the fish – but it was off again in a split second.

## WHERE TO START
Rutland is a vast expanse of water and can be daunting to even the most experienced of fly anglers.

Although its area measures approximately 3,300 acres, it can be split into three sections: the North Arm, South Arm and Main Basin. Still, local knowledge is key. I am very humbled by the fact I can count on both of the Barr brothers as not only fantastically gifted anglers but close friends as well and they both know this great expanse of water like the back of their hands. Being able to pick up the phone and find out where the fish are and what they are feeding on is great – all I need to do is to go out and catch them!

All of the wardens on Rutland are very knowledgeable of what's catching and where, so before you go out have a quick word with them to pick their brains. This is especially important if the weather has been settled for a few days; they will even be able to tell you about the likelihood of hatches and where to find them.

While I'm on the subject, settled weather is a must for consistent early season dry-fly fishing with shallower water a better bet, as it will heat up quicker.

## TALKING TACKLE
We already knew where the fish were, so setting up was the next job.

I set up with a 10ft 7-wt rod and a reel loaded with a floating Airflo Ridge line. I use a tiny Roman Moser braided loop on my line, which does not add any weight to the tip of my floater, helping it ride high in the water.

My leader set-up was a three-fly rig of approximately 18 feet of 4lb Drennan Ultragreen. Why? Simply because I've used it for years and am confident in it – therefore I only get smashed due to my own incompetence!

## FLIES AND FLOATANTS

My top-dropper fly was a size 12 Olive Half Hog Hopper. In the middle was a size 12 When All Else Fails (WAEF) black midge pattern and on the point was a Claret Half Hog Hopper, again a size 12.

This leader material floats so, to help take the shine off it and get it to sink, it's essential to apply a sinking agent like Orvis Mud to approx 18 inches either side of each fly.

I use Mucilin floatant on my flies as I don't like the tiny oily slicks coming from them that you get with some of the other floatants. To be honest, I grew up fishing dries on hill lochs for wild browns and never needed to use anything else – why change when you are

happy with what you have got?

As I mentioned earlier, the Half Hogs are flies that can be fished in or on the surface, depending on how much floatant is applied. The middle fly is only lightly coated and can be even more effective just under the surface so don't worry if it sinks – you will be surprised how many fish will take it!

## DRY-FLY APPROACH

So it was off to Manton we headed. Upon arrival we noticed how the wind was blowing offshore and there were clouds of midges seemingly dancing above the trees – always a good indication of the place to start.

We also noticed that the spent flies (the dying insects that have laid their eggs) were being blown out to the edge of the ripple where the hungry trout were picking them off easily.

Imitations fished static in this area were the most effective, as any movement at all was met with refusal.

With me fan casting and Stuart chucking it and chancing it, we steadily picked up fish drifting from the bank into open water. We also went looking for 'wind lanes' in the open water and picked up brown trout in them. Wind

## My methods of fishing dries from a drifting boat can be broken into two main types:

### 1 FAN CASTING

Cover all of the water in front of you, giving the flies no more than 15 seconds in one area, before lifting off and casting at a different angle. Fifteen seconds is long enough to give any trout the chance to take!

### 2 CHUCK IT AND CHANCE IT

Cast out your flies in front of the drifting boat. As your boat drifts onto them, slowly take up the slack line to keep in contact with them at all times.

The last few seconds before recasting are also important due to following fish not being able to make their minds up whether to eat them or not, but a slight increase in the speed of your flies is often enough to induce a take.

Incidentally, I have also found that it pays dividends not to strike hard but to lift your rod once the fish have taken your fly. This generally brings me many more successful hook-ups, especially when using 4lb tippet!

# Summer

lanes (calm channels on the surface) are areas in which, due to turbulence in the water, flies seem to get caught so there will obviously be trout in them too.

Later on in the day the hatch died off following a drop in air temperature and the fishing slowed. After moving down to New Zealand point, I changed my leader setup and went onto two small Half Hogs with a size 12 Booby on the top dropper. After casting, I tweaked the Booby through the waves with the small flies trailing behind.

We ended up landing and releasing another dozen or so fish, each coming to the small Booby and turning back onto the Hogs. The fish were still high enough in the surface but only switched back on when the Booby was making a wake going through the waves, drawing them to the disturbance.

Dry-fly fishing is a much-underrated technique when fishing on big reservoirs, so next time you go out, try putting up your spare rod with dries and give them a go. It's an excellent way of picking up quality fish and, with the right location and a little knowledge, it's easy to catch them!

You won't see a better-looking rainbow trout than this anywhere!

**RUTLAND WATER**

**Location:** Edith Weston, Rutland
**Open:** April 1st to December 31st (boats finish end of November)
**Tel:** 01780 686441
**Web:** www.anglianwaterleisure. co.uk

"It's an excellent way of picking up quality fish and, with the right location and a little knowledge, it's easy to catch them!"

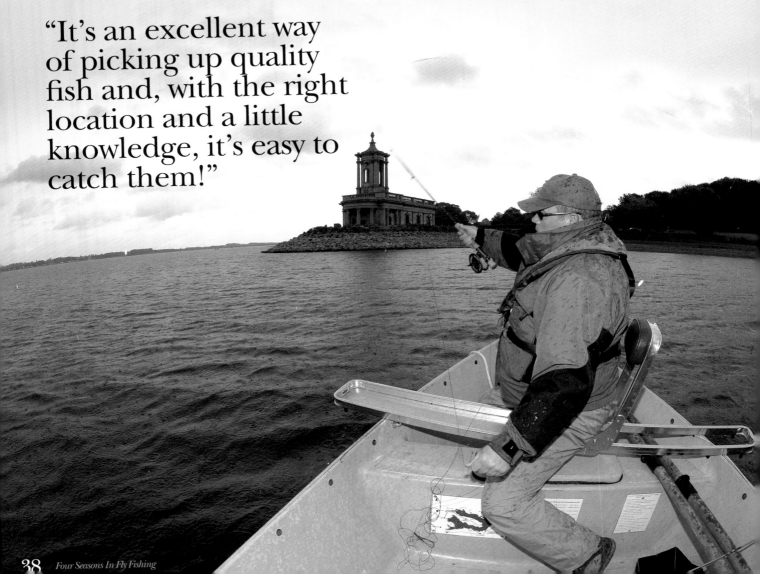

# 'FLY FISHING HOLIDAY BREAKS'

## OUTSTANDING VALUE AT ONLY £30 PER ANGLER PER DAY

### ADDITIONAL DAYS £25 per angler

Based on two anglers sharing a boat for three consecutive days or more fishing at our four prestigious fisheries all within 40 minutes drive.
Fishing includes the fishery bag limits each day plus catch and release.
There is a 10% discount on any tackle you buy at the Lodges during your stay.
Telephone the Fishing Lodge of your choice to book your holiday.

## Mix and match your venues

**Rutland Water** 01780 686441    **Grafham Water** 01480 810531
**Pitsford Water** 01604 781350    **Ravensthorpe** 01604 770875

### WHAT THE ANGLERS THOUGHT
*"Superb fishing for a great club outing
or holiday with a friend"*

love every drop
anglianwater

Visit our website for more details:
# www.anglianwater.co.uk/leisure

Prices could be subject to change.

# COPPER JIM

Fly fishing adventurer Andy Petherick shares an American nymph pattern that will change the way you fish, whether on still or running water.

I thought I would show off one of my top-secret flies.

I use the term 'my' very loosely. I cannot really take any of the credit for the pattern, even my version of it is not that far removed from the original. The reason for this feature is to share the pattern with readers and hope that it catches you some fish, I'm sure it will!

Gareth Jones, from Airflo, introduced me to the Copper John in early 2003.

I was aware of the pattern but had never fished with it, he was singing its praises to me, so I decided to tie a few and see what he was so excited about.

A quick search, via Google, bought up the original pattern developed by John Barr in the USA.

## A SIMPLER TYING

When I sat down at my tying bench I realised what a complex pattern it was. To be honest, I thought it was a bit overcomplicated for what

it was. I would imagine that on smaller hook sizes, 16 or less, it would be quite difficult to tie. This fact, coupled with the practicality that I didn't have the correct materials, meant that I decided to alter it a bit.

I had no goose biots, so I opted for pheasant tail. I decided against lead as an underbody, conscious of keeping the wire body level and even. I dug out some tungsten beads, Orvis do a good selection of sizes and colours, and decided to go with some copper ones for my first few flies.

The wire body was easy, and this led me to the thorax. Peacock herl gave just the look I was after. What I ended up with was part way between a Copper John and a Brassie.

I sat there wondering if the effort was worth it – I thought it was. I believe that fish look for triggers when they are hunting. By triggers I mean things that make an item instantly identifiable as a food item. Things like profile, legs, tails, being in the right place, anything that means it could be food.

# Summer

## ORIGINAL PATTERN

**Hook:** TMC 5262 or equivalent
**Thread:** Black 6/0
**Tail:** Brown goose biots
**Abdomen:** Copper wire
**Thorax:** Peacock herl
**Wing case:** Thin Skin, pearl Flashabou, and epoxy
**Legs:** Hungarian partridge or hen back or saddle
**Bead:** Brass
**Weight:** Lead wire

## COPPER JIM

**Hook:** To suit target invertebrate
**Tail:** Pheasant tail – coloured to match the body if possible
**Body:** Coloured UTC wire, in this case copper
**Head:** Copper tungsten bead
**Thorax:** Peacock herl

The Copper Jim is midway between a Brassie (top left) and a Copper John (bottom right)

I thought that the new version of the Copper John fitted the bill nicely. It had the profile of a waterborne nymph and the weight to get it where it should be – in front of the fish. I was quietly confident.

### COLOURED WIRES

Sometimes a fly pattern catches your attention, this one certainly got my creative juices flowing. Veniards distribute a range of wires by UTC, called Ultra Wire. They produce all sorts of colours, from copper and brown through to hot orange and chartreuse. With a selection of these at my disposal I did some serious tying that week, and tied up Copper Johns in all sizes and colours.

I couldn't really call it a Copper John, because it wasn't, so what should it be called? I didn't

have a name but a mate came up with the name Copper Jim – works for me!

The next time I went fishing I found out very quickly why Gareth got so excited about the pattern. It was early May and I was on a whistle-stop tour of the south, taking pictures for the magazine. I called in for a day with Darrin Barter on a little-known fishery in the heart of Hampshire – Horsebridge Springs. Located in the heart of the Test Valley, this is a real gem of a fishery run by the owner, Colin. For value for money, this place takes some beating. The fish are superb, and fight like demons, and Colin is a real character.

After a cup of coffee and a chat I set up my rod and walked over to a seat next to the lake to choose my first fly. It was peak mayfly time and about 9.30am. No adult flies were flying about but the fish were moving all over the place. I guessed that they were feeding on the active nymphs, so it was time to try the Copper Jim.

Initially I tied on a copper version. I had a take on the first cast but then things slowed. After about 10 minutes of sight casting to big rainbows and browns, and having them ignore my carefully presented offering, I decided to change. The Red Jims looked favourable so I decided to try one. I was glad I did.

> "The chartreuse and copper-coloured Jims proved to be the most effective. Between them they accounted for 23 fish that day."

The action was thick and fast on the first outing of the Red Jim.

### FLUFFED CAST

I was so excited by the fish I was seeing that I fluffed my first cast. I quickly stripped the line back and recast into the path of a big rainbow that had been tormenting me since I had arrived. The fly plopped down, about three feet in front of him; he swung around and nailed the Red Jim as if his life depended on it. I went on to catch two more fish in two casts.

All the commotion from my end of the lake drew the attention of Darrin, who was with me. He wandered over and asked what fly I was using and I showed him the Red Jims. I weakened to his puppy-dog look and gave him one to try. He went away and instantly started to catch. That day proved the power of the Jim on stillwaters, but would it work on rivers as

A slow retrieve on a floating line proved irresistible.

Phill Parker gets in on the Copper Jim action at Horsebridge Springs.

the original John does? Indeed, this is what the pattern was developed for.

## PERFECT TEST

During the same trip I was lucky enough to have the opportunity to fish a beat on the Itchen that is loaded with grayling. This would be the perfect test for my hot new property. This time the chartreuse and copper-coloured Jims proved to the most effective. Between them they accounted for 23 fish that day.

This started me thinking. The colour of the fly was playing a major part in its success. In theory it should be matched to the most abundant invertebrate colour for best results.

## WORDS FROM THE ORIGINAL'S CREATOR

I remembered something that I had seen on the website I had originally visited and went back for a second look. What follows is an extract:

"With so many colours of wire available, it can be hard to choose what colour Copper John to fish. When in doubt, the copper-wire Copper John is a good choice. For years that was all Barr used, and the colour is no less effective now that there are more colours to choose from.

"At times it pays to show fish many colours, to see which one works, but you can also match the size and colour of the Copper John to insects that have been, are, or will be emerging. Barr believes that insects don't have to be present for fish to key in on a particular colour or size.

Copper and chartreuse were the top colours — taking 23 grayling in one outing!

"If it ain't chartreuse, it ain't no use."

"For instance, he has found a correlation between caddis activity and the colour green. If your area has a good population of free-living caddis, such as Rhyacophila, a green Copper John is a good candidate. In the spring, Barr will often reach for a green Copper John first.

"Chartreuse wire only became available last year, it hasn't been thoroughly tested, but all reports suggest it works well as a caddis imitation and general attractor. Lefty Kreh says: 'If it ain't chartreuse, it ain't no use.' The colour seems to have universal appeal to fish species, but freshwater anglers have been slower to catch on than their saltwater brethren. (A little known fact is that chartreuse is the most visible colour under water at distance, maybe that's why the Cat's Whisker is so effective?)"

### TRY IT IN BLUE

"Lately, the colour blue has created a commotion on trout streams in Colorado. Barr recalls a conversation with John Randolph, editor of Fly Fisherman. This was regarding the effectiveness of Charlie Meck's dry fly, the Patriot, which incorporates blue Krystal Flash in the body.

"Meck came up with the idea after reading a study about how rainbow trout in particular respond positively to the colour blue. The Patriot seems to pull trout up when nothing else will and the blue Copper John has produced similar results.

"Barr also created the silver Copper John for

a reason. He often observed schools of fathead minnows in bass ponds near his home. He noticed that when there isn't good light, and he couldn't really see the fish at all, each time a minnow turned it looked like miniature flash bulbs, little glints of light.

"He developed the silver Copper to imitate the turning of scales that might trigger a grab. Barr says: 'Silver is the glint of a baitfish, which might trigger strikes. It's a reaction bait. Does a spinnerbait look like a shad? I think the Copper Johns generally get a lot of reaction strikes. Fish don't try to find something wrong with your pattern; they look for something right with it. Fish don't think things over before they bite.'"

### PAIR THE SIZE OF FLY WITH THE DEPTH OF WATER

"You should correlate the size of your Copper John with the depth of the water you are fishing. Use a large Copper John to get your fly down in deep water and a small Copper if you are fishing in skinny water. Barr also tries to correlate the size of the Copper with the size of mayfly nymphs, but if he needs to get his fly down, he fine-tunes the hatch matching with the dropper."

Taking this into account, I believe that the Jim or the John has a lot of potential, in different colours and sizes. I agree with what John wrote on the website and think the pattern will excel on rivers and stillwaters. Blue... now there's an interesting theory...

# A LITTLE STIMULATION

Not all American imports prove to be popular here in the UK, says George Barron, but the Stimulator, albeit tweaked versions of it, can work wonders on our wild trout!

When it comes to prospecting patterns the Stimulator can be a really good first choice.

"Have a nice day!" When you think about it, there are a lot of things that we Brits have to thank America for. To name but a few, there was good old Donald Duck, Elvis Presley, Coca-Cola, hamburgers and, I think the guy said: "Dolly Parton's greatest hits!" Oh, and winning the Second World War.

From a fishing perspective, there are not that many American fly patterns that have actually crossed the Atlantic and survived in their created form.

Even Don Gapen's original Muddler Minnow has been bastardised almost to extinction to produce so many hybrid, mini and scaled-down versions to suit British angling requirements. One or two other patterns have kicked around the fringes, such as the Humpy, but in reality most American patterns have created more initial novelty value for fly-tying demonstrators than have actually proved to be out-and-out means of catching fish. (With reference to fish in this feature, I mean wild brown trout, not put-and-take rainbows.)

However, one exception when it comes to fooling wild trout has been that relatively recent arrival, the Stimulator. Apparently, in the States it effectively imitates a large number of caddis-type back-wing flies – sedges to you and me – stoneflies and various other terrestrials. In the raw it's a big ugly looking, overdressed, multi-coloured dry fly that works very well on the big turbulent rivers during the full term of the American fishing season. Best colours over there seem to be tans and olives, though, similar to 'casual dress' American shirts. Loud colours such as orange, yellow and grey also have their day, albeit you might have to add rubber legs... I kid you not.

While conventional 'US of A' Stimulator dressings might create some interest when fished singularly as a 'ginked-up' dry fly, the alternative patterns – and more interesting as far as UK angling is concerned – will more likely be cloned wet flies.

There is a great misconception that most Irish wet flies are big bushy things; this could be the case in America too because, while many of their Stimulator patterns are big and bushy, a great majority of their most successful flies are tied in sizes 12 to 16. Solely from a wet-fly perspective, American-dressed Stimulators to my mind could never effectively be retrieved on a conventional wet-fly cast without twisting and spinning on the leader. I accept the fly was never intended to be pulled but I'm merely setting the scene to justify the relatively scaled-down patterns that I loosely refer to as Stimulators in the UK.

I first played around with wet-fly variations of Stimulators about eight years ago and a couple of my early patterns were actually quite successful. As always with my own patterns they are tied using mostly hen hackles and a Dabbler-like tail to balance the fly, but were made up a wee bit lighter with the amount of deer hair I used in the wing than on most other modern dressings.

At that time anglers, certainly in Ireland, were only just wising up to the fact that wild brownies were catchable on overcast days during the summer months in deeper water. These fish would follow the daphnia to the upper layers and be feeding at a time of year when, previously, tradition said we should give daytime fishing a miss.

The first pattern that worked for me I christened the SNOT fly – after a lovely town called 'Smell-no-Taste' in Liberia, West Africa, where I was drinking in a shanty bar one night and was almost bitten to death by something about the same size and shape as the tying. The base colour here is traditionally dark Irish and it always seems like retribution when a trout takes this fly, sort of payback time.

Into a good fighting fish out in open water on Wales' Lake Vyrnwy.

The other early Stimulator that got me a few tugs was a far gaudier creation from the other end of the Irish colour spectrum, golden olive being the dominant factor so as to conform to brighter fishing conditions. Lough Melvin, straddling the border between the north and south in Ireland, and at that time seemingly holding a far greater head of free-rising 'black trout' or sonoghan than at present, was a great venue for sport with this fly and also the 'mighty Mask'.

Naming flies can be a boring exercise at times but I like to give them 'proper' handles that remind me of nice times in my life. This one I dedicated, with her kind permission, to Judy, the wife of Dr E J (Ted) Malone, a great fly-tying hero of mine, and called it the Mrs Malone. It's a lovely looking fly, full of life and colour like the lady herself, and deserving of being tied with the finest of materials.

Things have moved on a wee bit Stimulator-wise in the last few years. Bulk seems to have given way to more thinned-down and, to an extent, more lifelike patterns, certainly on the Western Loughs where the water clarity is excellent and the natural food larder is plentiful.

I think, with due respect to the fish, most wet-fly patterns should at least bear a passing resemblance to something lifelike, if only in colour and mobility. I'd been playing around with some new piscatorial works of art, loosely associated with Stimulator patterns, since the tail end of last season and obviously only time and trout will show how effective they are, but I'm quietly optimistic about them. I like utilitarian wet-fly patterns, flies that cover more than one option for me when pulling a three or four-fly cast loch-style from a drifting boat, be it over shallows or daphnia-rich deeper water.

The make-up is classic wet fly holding a mix of traditional Irish colours, plus a concentration of 'hotspots' at the rear end in the form of tags or tails and other bright extras. The profile is lighter than the first two patterns but retains a few distinctive features that might excite trout during olive, mayfly or even sedge hatches and the addition of a deer-hair wing in various colours gives the fly dresser many options to play around with.

I used these patterns as my template for demonstrating during my two days in

## GALWAY LIGHT OLIVE

**Hook:** Fulling Mill Competition Heavyweight, sizes 10 and 12
**Tag:** Chartreuse holographic tinsel
**Tail:** Bunch natural pheasant-tail fibres
**Rib:** UTC small hot yellow wire
**Body:** Golden olive seal's fur
**First hackle:** Four turns golden olive hen
**Wing:** Bleached coastal deer hair
**Front hackle:** Four turns of longish medium olive hen

## SNOT FLY

**Hook:** Fulling Mill Competition Heavyweight, sizes 10 and 12
**Tail:** A bunch of pheasant tail, dyed claret
**Rib:** Red UTC wire
**Body:** Rear – pearly over black thread; front – dark claret seal's fur
**Body hackle:** Claret hen
**Wing:** Bleached coastal deer hair
**Head hackle:** Three or four turns of longish grizzle hen

## GALWAY CLARET

**Hook:** Fulling Mill Competition Heavyweight, sizes 10 and 12
**Tail:** Under-tail tippets dyed red; over-tail, bunch natural pheasant tail fibres.
**Rib:** Fine silver wire
**Body:** Pearly holographic over black thread
**First hackle:** Four turns of dark claret hen
**Wing:** Dyed claret deer hair
**Front hackle:** Four turns longish greenwell hen

attendance at the highly successful Irish Fly Fair in Galway last November, where they raised a fair bit of local interest. For want of a better name I refer to them simply as the Galway flies; in construction they lend themselves to be adapted for almost all circumstances, even a spot of salmon or sea-trout fishing from a boat.

Depending on hook size, with or without a bunch of deer hair, muntjac or even polar bear wing they will be a wee bit different from the bog-standard wets normally thrown at wild brownies. Meaty flies can look out of balance without a tail of sorts and with the Galway flies I've actually taken it a step further and included a double tail, basically for two reasons – pheasant-tail fibres are the first thing to disappear from a dabbler after a few fish, so the addition of tippets underneath ensures that, even if the fibres get nipped off the fly is still fishable, and the second tail gives an opportunity to add an extra colour or hotspot to the dressing without creating something too gaudy.

The Galway Copper is good for early season and towards the later part of the year when the trout get into aggressive mating mood. Maybe best suited to peaty waters but with enough light-bouncing qualities about it to wind up a few Midlands rainbows.

A scaled-down version of the SNOT fly with less bulk and some other refinements is the Galway Claret, a great fly on overcast and mucky days when the trout seem to take a shine to claret. I'm not averse to sticking it on the tail in a bit of a blow. As with the Copper version, I like the effect of stark colour being blown through the hackles by the use of holographic tinsel along the body of the fly. In a size 12 I'd fish this pattern for rainbows on some of higher-lying waters like Brenig and Clywedog.

Various shades of olive would be the choice of most anglers heading for the very fertile Irish loughs at most times during the season. I prefer light olive shades on the brighter days and darker hues when there is a bit of cloud cover, with butts and ribbing as the cosmetic additions to enhance and give the necessary wee bit of kick. The utilitarian Galway Light Olive should be useful enough to see service during both olive and Mayfly hatches.

The traditional Extractor is a very good fly come the start of the Mayfly hatch, certainly in the more northern waters. I can only think that's because when the beast is at the point of hatch there is a burst of blood during metamorphosis that appears highly attractive to feeding trout. I've jazzed up the pattern with a wet stimulator look, making it a more obvious pick for the top-dropper position, rather than as an out-and-out point fly.

> "I like the effect of stark colour being blown through the hackles by the use of holographic tinsel along the body of the fly."

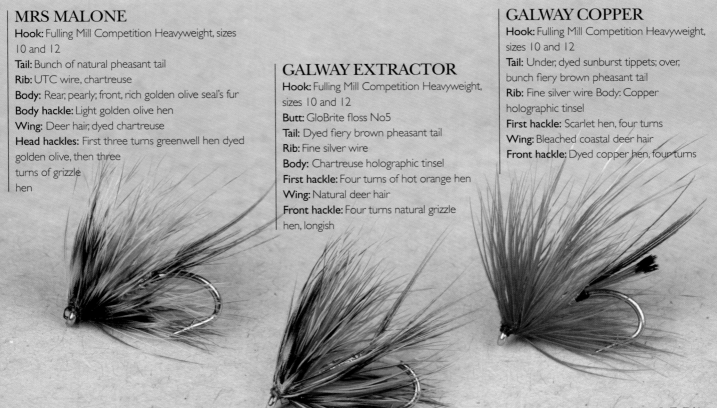

### MRS MALONE

**Hook:** Fulling Mill Competition Heavyweight, sizes 10 and 12
**Tail:** Bunch of natural pheasant tail
**Rib:** UTC wire, chartreuse
**Body:** Rear, pearly; front, rich golden olive seal's fur
**Body hackle:** Light golden olive hen
**Wing:** Deer hair, dyed chartreuse
**Head hackles:** First three turns greenwell hen dyed golden olive, then three turns of grizzle hen

### GALWAY EXTRACTOR

**Hook:** Fulling Mill Competition Heavyweight, sizes 10 and 12
**Butt:** GloBrite floss No5
**Tail:** Dyed fiery brown pheasant tail
**Rib:** Fine silver wire
**Body:** Chartreuse holographic tinsel
**First hackle:** Four turns of hot orange hen
**Wing:** Natural deer hair
**Front hackle:** Four turns natural grizzle hen, longish

### GALWAY COPPER

**Hook:** Fulling Mill Competition Heavyweight, sizes 10 and 12
**Tail:** Under, dyed sunburst tippets; over, bunch fiery brown pheasant tail
**Rib:** Fine silver wire Body: Copper holographic tinsel
**First hackle:** Scarlet hen, four turns
**Wing:** Bleached coastal deer hair
**Front hackle:** Dyed copper hen, four turns

# NYMPHING FOR
# BARBEL

**John** Stephens uses the art of Czech and French
Nymphing to land his first-ever fly-caught barbel.

After several months working in Stuttgart, on the edge of Germany's famous Black Forest, I finally found time to fulfil a vow to myself and sample some of the excellent fly fishing the region has to offer. I packed my travel rod in the boot of the car and headed south to meet a man who could really show me the ropes – tackle-shop owner and guide Ruediger Kopf.

Ruediger offers fishing excursions in the Black Forest and also in neighbouring France and Switzerland. An expert in Czech and French Nymph techniques he has also developed a penchant for what he calls 'the freshwater bonefish'... the barbel.

On this trip Ruediger promised to show me how to approach and catch this elusive yet potentially pulse-racing quarry.

I met him at his tackle shop in Merdingen, which was the ideal place for him to show me some of the specialist flies he uses for these muscle-packed coarse fish, while explaining something of the water where they are to be found and the conditions needed to take them on the fly.

FLOW

### PERFECT PRESENTATION
By raising the rod tip just as the flies are approaching the fish, the patterns rise in the water, inducing the barbel to take.

## RUEDIGER KOPF'S BARBEL FLIES

HVK CASED CADDIS

THE CONDOM

CZECH NYMPH SPEZIAL

CZECH NYMPH

FRENCH NYMPH

John Stephens, into a big barbel, has to react fast to get some line back on the reel.

## "Then, just as he raises the rod once more, a barbel dives forward and the dropper fly disappears."

"Barbel are bottom feeders, their mouths designed to root among the stones and gravel of the riverbed," he said. "The flies that I find work best are weighted caddis-type patterns tied on tungsten-bead jig hooks. I mainly use size 8 or 10. The jig hook ensures that the fly travels over the riverbed point up, reducing the chances of snagging on the bottom. This is an important feature in the design fo the fly, since you want it to bounce along the bottom and not get caught up on anything.

"I fish a two-fly cast, with this fly on the top dropper and a smaller weighted caddis or Czech Nymph pattern on the point. I also use Czech and French Nymphs, especially when the fish are proving to be more selective and taking smaller bugs.

"You'll need a rod that will handle these fish. I would recommend a 7-wt or 8-wt rod with a reel that has a decent clutch or drag system. A floating line is fine, but make sure you have plenty of backing loaded; these fish can run and run. I use a 10lb tapered leader needle knotted to the fly line with three feet of 8lb to 10lb fluorocarbon tippet. This setup will turn over the weighted flies when fishing a long line."

Ruediger's favourite location, and the one he is taking me to, is on the Old Rhine, at a stretch near the town of Hartheim.

There are barbel on many rivers in Germany but if you want to catch them on a fly you must find not only the right river, but the correct stretch coupled with the perfect conditions. Look for a river that is fairly shallow, fast-flowing, with a stone and gravel bed and a good weed growth, which will indicate a plentiful supply of the nymphs and bugs that barbel love to feast on. Areas where the pace of the river slows into a pool, where you find gravel beaches or where the deeper channels lie are the most likely fish-holding areas.

There are some good spots on the Old Rhine and the fish tend to have an average size of 3lb to 4lb. They aren't found everywhere on the river, only in particular runs, and that's why you need a good guide like Ruediger.

After a short drive from his tackle shop we arrive at the wide, smooth-flowing river, very similar in looks to some parts of the River Wye around Hereford.

The stretch we have opted for is fairly shallow and boulder-strewn with good water clarity – excellent for spotting those long olive-coloured fish.

After a few moments Ruediger points out a group of large fish finning in the current about 15 metres from where we are standing. Five metres below them is another shoal – the river seems full of them; the more I look the more I see moving gently in the current.

We tackle up and wade out into the river.

Ruediger Kopf with a double-figure barbel taken on his favourite Barbel Heavyweight.

It's tricky going; the boulders are large and silted, so you have to be careful where you place your feet. I watch as Ruediger throws a line up and across, five or six metres above the fish. The flies sink quickly and he holds the rod tip up, allowing the flies to tumble down over the stony bottom toward the shoal. I can see the fish gently finning, moving from side to side and rooting around among the stones. Occasionally there's a telltale flash as a fish intercepts something that's been dislodged.

As the flies drift towards the leading fish, Ruediger lifts the rod tip. This causes his heavily weighted dropper to rise three or four inches off the bottom and for the point fly to flutter over the riverbed.

He then lowers it again, allowing the flies to settle back among the silt and stones. He repeats the action as the flies move closer to the fish. Then, just as he raises the rod once more, a barbel dives forward and the dropper fly disappears. Ruediger lifts the rod and the fish is on!

His rod bends alarmingly and the line zips out across the river as the fish powers off toward the opposite bank. The initial surge is impressive and some serious side strain is needed to gain control.

The barbel turns and moves diagonally back toward us. Ruediger wades further out to get behind the fish. He wants to stop it from getting beneath him where he would have to play it against the current; although not fast here, it still gives the fish an advantage. The rod arcs over again and the fish runs up river. With some judicious application of welly, a pristine power-packed barbel nudging 7lb is finally brought to the net.

It looks like a torpedo, with a huge, low-slung mouth designed for hoovering the riverbed and

## RK BARBEL HEAVYWEIGHT

**Hook:** Knapek Jig, sizes 4 to 12 **Thread:** UNI Thread 6/0, black
**Weight:** Tungsten bead
**Body materials:** Dubbing mix of Antron (20%), deer hair (10%) and hare (70%) – olive (abdomen), brown (thorax)

**1** Place the hook in the vice and run the thread down to just past the hook point.

**2** Tie in the lead wire or tungsten lace so that it lies along the top of the hook, forming a keel.

**3** Take the thread back down the hook and double the lace over. Tie it down, then run the thread back along the hook to lock the lace in.

**4** Trim off the excess lace and apply varnish to secure it in position.

**5** Apply dubbing to the thread and dub along the hook, stopping short of the eye to allow a collar of darker dubbing.

**6** Apply dark brown or claret dubbing to the thread and take three turns around the hook to produce a dark collar.

**7** Whip finish, locking the thread down behind the eye. Apply a touch of varnish.

This is a great barbel fly that is very easy to tie. It can be tied in a range of colours. In my tying I have used an ordinary gold head bead with a keel of tungsten lace to help the fly to fish point up - I prefer to use tungsten lace or sheet rather than lead, since in some countries lead is banned.

# Summer

"The method used to catch barbel on the fly is very simple yet very effective and I reckon it may well work on rivers in the UK."

Take great care with these fish to revive them, as they give their all in the fight.

mopping up those rock-hugging bugs. It has taken the fly with confidence and some delicate work with the forceps is needed to extract the barbless hook. Ruediger holds the fish by the tail for a moment until it revives and swims off to rejoin its mates.

Now it is my turn. I follow Ruediger's technique, allowing the flies to sink and then lifting the rod so that I stay in contact with them as they travel along the riverbed.

I slowly lift then lower the rod tip to move the flies, and I watch excitedly as a fish on the far side of the pod moves up and across to intercept the fly.

There is a flash of white – I lift and... bang, the fly is snatched away and line strips out from the reel as the barbel powers off downriver with Ruediger screaming at me to go after it while I keep the rod well up in the air.

I obey his command while stumbling over the boulders and holding on to my fish. I am down to the backing and it is still going. Then it stops. I move on, taking up slack line. There is no further movement, the fish just lies there like a log on the bottom of the river.

I keep moving until I'm just below it. Then I put on some pressure and that does the trick because the fish jets off once again at full throttle before I can finally bully it to the net.

The power needed to tame the fish – at 6lb it's slightly smaller than Ruediger's – leaves me nursing a sore arm. But my first-ever barbel on the fly is well worth the pain.

Through the rest of the day we fish two more stretches of the river and have half a dozen more fish, one of which measures just under 60 centimetres.

The method used to catch barbel on the fly is very simple yet very effective and I reckon it may well work on rivers in the UK. I'll certainly be giving it a go come the summer.

## LICENCES AND PERMITS

Fishing in Germany is highly regulated and in order to fish you must first obtain a Fischereischein, the German state fishing licence.

Then you need a fishing permit or day ticket for the particular stretch of water you intend to fish.

## FACT FILE
Old Rhine River, Hartheim, Germany
**Contact:** Ruediger Kopf
**E-mail:** rkopf@black-forest-flyfishing.de
**www**.black-forest-flyfishing.de

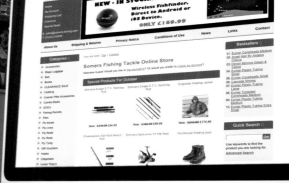

# KINGFISHER DAMSEL

**The Kingfisher** Damsel is relatively new but this electrifying pattern incorporates even more blue, great when the adult flies are on the go.

**Hook:** Fulling Mill Short Shank Special, size 6
**Bead:** Hanak, metallic blue, 3mm
**Thread:** Olive Semperfli
**Tail:** Olive marabou, with a few strands of Aqua Tinsel either side
**Rib:** Aqua Holographic
**Body:** Dubbed marabou
**Hackle:** Green partridge

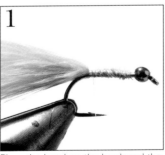

**1** Place the bead on the hook and the hook in the vice. Attach a generous hank of marabou to the hook for the tail and trim waste.

**2** Tie in the Aqua tinsel on either side of the tail and also catch in the ribbing material at the rear of the hook.

**3** Create quite a thick dubbing rope from the olive marabou and wind it up the body in close-touching turns, stopping behind the eye.

**4** Wind the Aqua Holographic up the hook shank in nice, even open turns stopping just behind the bead; trim excess.

**5** Attach the hackle by the tips and wind around the hook shank twice, secure with thread. Create a fine dubbing rope and wind as a collar.

**6** Before whip finishing add a drop of varnish to the thread, whip finish and trim waste.

# AUTUMN

As things start to cool down the fish, all of them, are
on the fin and ready to feed before the onset of winter.

# SURF'S UP

**With** more of us trying our hand at saltwater fly fishing, Steve Cullen looks at how anyone can get in on the act for some awesome seaside action.

Saltwater fly fishing has been around for a very long time now and it's growing in popularity. Bass have often been the main target but anglers are also trying their hands at the very shy and extremely difficult to catch mullet.

Mullet are tough customers at the best of times, but to fool them using fly imitations offers an even greater challenge and higher reward when your plan finally comes together. There are a few very good anglers out there who have been honing their techniques over the last few years, and indeed their fly patterns in order to succeed with these unbelievably tricky fish, but can your average flyfisher catch one?

Glen Pointon and I are heading out into 'the salt' in the hope that we can get among some bass, and indeed mullet. Although we've tied up some pretty random fly patterns for the mullet – everything from little nymphs to seaweed imitations – our fly gear is pretty much what we use for our stillwater fishing.

## TACKLE FOR THE SALT

A 10ft 7-wt fly rod with a fast action is best as at times you'll be turning over biggish flies – we're talking bass here – and often into a headwind.

Reels need to be robust but nothing too fancy. I just use my Vision Koma – the thing is pretty much indestructible. It can carry a lot of backing, which may well be needed, and the drag is reliable. It's also a large-arbor model so I can retrieve my fly line fast, should I have to.

The fly line that you're likely to use is the humble floater, and in fact there's really no need for anything else. Any kind of sinking line is a hindrance where waves are concerned; they will just sink or get tangled in your feet.

Flies can be anything that you want to try: Shrimps, Diawl Bachs, wet flies with soft hackles and even things that resemble weed will work for the mullet. Bass are more eager takers and will fall for most flies, from White Woolly Buggers to the ever-popular Clouser Minnow.

Fishing in saltwater has become more refined, with better tackle and techniques helping us catch more species, more successfully. Bass are not too tricky on the fly, in fact schoolies are pretty much suicidal at times.

Mullet, on the other hand, are super tough and I'm convinced that catching them is more about luck than skill.

## MEGA-TRICKY MULLET

The best time to target mullet is when they are feeding, so locating these fish is half the battle. Although they are easy to spot, the problem is when you see them basking or cruising they will rarely take a fly. It's in the shallows that they will avidly feed and this is when they can be successfully targeted with a fly.

It helps if there is a little bit of wave to give them some cover from above, as it makes them more confident. Keeping still is important – if you stand stock still and wait for the fish to come to you, they can remain so confident in their feeding that they will actually bump into your legs or swim between them.

Glen Pointon was quick to get in on the bass action; his Clouser was a big hit and the key to catching was getting it to fish on the outside of the fast water.

Having a kayak means you can cover far more water; it's also very handy for fishing deeper areas where you can't wade.

## SUPER-AGGRESSIVE BASS

Look for a large intertidal movement of water and you'll be sure to find bass hunting here on the incoming tide. Shallow, rocky reefs or long, sandy beaches with the odd gulley in among them are what you're after!

As mentioned they are hunters, so unlike the slow deliberate approach that you'd use with mullet, the casting and indeed presentation can be quite crude when you're after these fish. Cast your line out far and roly-poly or strip retrieve to get some movement in your flies and try and appeal to the aggressive nature of bass. It's speculative fishing; try and cover water and hunt your fish down.

Bass are true predators and will pretty much have a go at anything that happens to be in their way, whether it swims, crawls or wriggles. They especially like crabs, sandeels and small shoaling fish like mackerel, which tend to be the staple diet of this voracious hunter. You must think about this when you're targeting them, most fish-type lures are worth a go and can be a real hit with the bass.

## FOUR MILE BRIDGE

Glen has fished the Four Mile Bridge in Anglesey before; he knows it has features that appeal to both mullet and the bass and where they are, so it saves us a whole lot of hassle.

It is an amazing place to fish as the sea is squeezed through a very narrow area; at its narrowest the water is pushed up and through the bridge, creating a very strong current either side as the tide ebbs and flows. Looking down from the bridge you'll see mullet – big ones too – and you'll also witness bass jumping in the fast flow as the tide pushes in and out. There's nothing better than being able to see fish to get your confidence up!

## HANDY KAYAK

There's a kayak shop in the nearby village and I hire one at £25 for the day, although Glen has his own. The benefits of having the kayaks is that we can head south, stop at a wide sandbank and then follow the tide as it comes in. Then we can track the mullet as they feed their way up the sandbank eating mud shrimps as they go.

In a half-hour paddle down we see very little fish activity; we spook a few mullet but Glen mentions that the last time he was here the number of fish that he saw was incredible, far more than we had spotted.

As the tide starts to come in we head back up toward the bridge – it's far easier paddling with the tide! The water is starting to rush through the gap in the bridge, heading north, so we get out of the kayaks and head for the water coming through the other side.

We cast some sizeable Clousers into the fast water, looking to get one of the many bass we see sporting in the current to take.

## HITTING THE FLATS

It proves fruitless, though, as the water is bombing through now and we can't fish the flies properly, so it's back into the kayaks and up to the flats near two little islands. There's deep water at the end of the flats and we can see mullet coming up on to the shallow water.

Talk about exciting! We see huge fish coming into the low water, sending up plumes of spray as they do so in the warm shallows. Others are more measured, slipping over and slowly making their way up with the bow waves and their tails giving them away. These ones, we guess are feeding.

## SOFT TOUCH IN THE SEA

Glen is on the case straightaway, casting his Soft-Touch Shrimp with gusto at these fish.

## MUST DO'S

- Check the tides
- Always wear a lifejacket
- Don't go out alone
- Take a mobile phone
- Have plenty of water
- Use sun block
- Wear glasses and a hat
- Wear appropriate footwear

Nothing fancy is required for a trip to the sea – your normal reservoir gear will do just fine, but make sure that you rinse it thoroughly with freshwater afterwards.

I go for a different approach, having been told that small salmon flies like a Curry's Shrimp can work wonders when roly-poly retrieved past the noses of these feeding fish.

However, after 30 minutes of seeing every mullet I cast at bolting in the opposite direction from my fly, I realise that it's not going to work for me.

## IMPOSSIBLE FISH

Glen is equally frustrated: "These things are super sensitive and I've been through my fly box – what the hell can we do? I've never known fish to be so bloody spooky!"

I decide to swap my setup round, taking off the 8lb fluoro and going down to 6lb, using a 10ft leader with my team of Mullet Spiders two feet apart on the last four feet!

I want my fly patterns to be easy to take; the little whisps of feathers are unobtrusive, they don't stand out and they won't scare these super-duper-spooky fish.

## NERVOUS WATER

The water level is rising and the splashy fish we saw earlier are nowhere to be seen. Now it's just swirls and several sipping at the surface every now and again, but when a big shoal moves through the sea shimmers – it's like 'nervous' water.

I've made about a thousand casts and have pretty much given up hope... until I get a take. When it comes it's almost imperceptible, but then it's running, running hard with line ripping through my fingers as it takes off on a searing dash and I watch as 50 yards of line disappear through the rod rings!

Straightaway I try and play the fish off the reel and use the drag to keep tension on it, trying to keep everything smooth. Mullet

# DNA CLOUSER

**Hook:** Jardine F222, size 6
**Thread:** White 6/0 Eyes: Real Eyes Plus, 4mm, red. After tying, use Bug-Bond or epoxy between the eyes
**Wing:** Holo Fusion Polar over Holo Fusion dark olive DNA

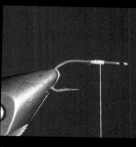

**1** Attach some thread to the centre of the hook.

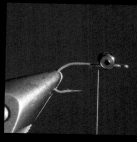

**2** Now attach the eyes with figure-of-eight thread wraps until they are locked in place.

**3** Secure the Polar DNA at the top of the hook shank and trim waste in front of the eyes.

**4** Bring the thread under the eyes and take several tight thread wraps over the DNA to secure in place.

**5** Turn the vice jaws round 180 degrees and then attach the dark olive DNA.

**6** Secure behind the eyes. Trim the DNA to length and finally use Bug-Bond between the eyes for extra security.

actually have quite tough mouths and those lips offer a great hook-hold, so I'm only worried about the other flies fouling weed.

## BRITISH BONES

I've caught bonefish and I have to say that this little mullet is doing a very good impression of one! Two solid runs later and with Glen running to get the camera from my neck – he'd followed a shoal of huge fish and was about 100 yards away, knee deep in thick mud when I hooked it – I beach it.

It's a stunner: a golden mullet, the gold spot behind its eye lit up by the high afternoon sun. It's a beautiful looking fish... but it's small. I was convinced it was going to be three times bigger and can only imagine what a big one goes like!

## BACK TO THE BRIDGE

With the water level now too high and the mullet having pretty much stopped feeding, and indeed showing, we head back to the bridge. Sitting on it, looking over, we see the slow change as the water stops moving through the arch and everything becomes still. There's no movement, no sound... it's quiet.

Then, slowly at first but quickly building, the flow starts going back the way it came, heading south, and as it does the bass start to show!

## INTO THE CARNAGE

Quick as a flash Pointon scrabbles down the other side, jumps into the kayak and gets into position to the left of the flow. I head down to the shallow bottom end of the pool and wade out up to thigh depth. From here I can cast into the tail end of the flow.

Glen whacks out his Clouser and after just a couple of casts, shouts down to me: "Bass!" This is quickly followed by "B\*\*\*\*\*\*, it's off."

No matter, next cast and he's in again! He soon has it in, a small schoolie about 12oz! He follows it up with a bigger one and then another, even bigger. The hectic sport continues for about 20 minutes as he hooks, drops or lands bass after bass, one of which, his biggest, coughs up two little crabs!

I don't fare so well. Having left my kayak I can't get near the action but I take a couple of little silver beauties before the feeding frenzy subsides – jeez do they fight!

Between the two of us we manage a decent haul of fish – 12 bass and one golden mullet – and all on the standard gear we'd normally use on stillwaters.

If you're heading to the coast with the family this year, throw some gear in the car – catching fish in saltwater is far easier than you'd think!

**MULLET SPIDER**
**Hook:** Tiemco 2487BL, size 12
**Body:** Chartreuse ostrich herl
**Rib:** Tying thread
**Hackle:** Partridge, dyed olive

Yee-ha! Nailed it! The toughest fish in the UK on the fly? I'd say so – I'd describe the mullet as 'the fish of a thousand casts'!

# SALT WATER FISHING
## SPECIALISTS

at selection of lines, flies & hooks

ver 200+ rods & reels

**WE HAVE OFFERS ON ROD & REEL COMBOS**

We have everything for the salt water angler, with a massive selection of rods, reels, lines, flies, fly-tying equipment, wire, hooks, waders & clothing.

*We are the main dealers for*

PENN • MAKAIRA • SALMO • ABU • SAVAGE • LOOP • SIMMS • SCOTT RODS • HARDY & GREYS • ABEL • NAUTILUS • CORTLAND
GUIDELINE • ORVIS • LAMSON • TEMPLE FORK • FULLING MILL • TURRALL • RIO • SPARTON • MONTANA FLY • WHITING • VENIARD
METZ • FUNKY • TIEMCO • MCLEAN • UTC • UN • CARRON FLY LINES • C & F • REGAL • HAYABUSA • COSTA DEL MAR • VISION
SNOWBEE • PARTRIDGE • KAMASAN • WYCHWOOD • H2O • FAP • FOXY-TAILS • SCIERRA • SONIC • ATLAS • SAGE PLUS MANY MORE...

**Follow us on**

**Unit 22, Robinsons Industrial Est, Shaftesbury St, Derby, DE23 8NL**
Tel. 01332 331548 // www.game-anglingconsultancy.com

# FRESHWATER CROCS

WWW.GUIDEDFISHING.INFO

Use big flies to provoke a response from big pike.

# 35LB PIKE ON THE FLY

**After** years of study, Andy Bowman now has a great way of knowing when to target BIG pike, our top freshwater predator!

Fast and furious action can be expected when you're in the Optimal Temperature Zone.

When I first started fishing for pike with a fly, I couldn't work out why these supposedly 'easy to catch' fish would often send me home empty-handed and with more questions than answers. The general view was that pike are voracious beasts that spend most of their time continually and indiscriminately attacking whatever they found in front of their noses.

Nothing could be further from the truth.

I have been fishing for pike since boyhood, mainly around the Loch Lomond area, rambling over the moors and farmland to reach beautiful shallow, green and verdant bays.

I hunted the many predators that sunned themselves near the surface. I caught many pike, but never thought they were suicidal. Voracious, yes, but only when the time was right.

I've also been a flyfisher from a young age and experience has taught me about the kind of conditions that increase or decrease the chances of success with game fish.

I learned about high, low, clear and dirty water, spate rivers, huge lochs, tiny ones, big waves, flat calms and a whole lot more. All good stuff, to be stored and recycled. Much of that information has since been employed in search of pike on the fly.

Salmon anglers cite 7°C (45F) as the magic number at which a salmon will rise to a fly near the surface. They can, of course, be caught in much lower temperatures, using sinking lines, but they could never be called 'free rising' in those conditions.

The best taking temperature band for free-rising salmon would probably be 7°C to 15°C. I wondered what, if anything, were the magic numbers in pike fly fishing?

## INVALUABLE DATA

Ten years ago I started meticulously recording the details of every pike fishing trip I made and in particular the air and water temperatures. Wind, weather and times of day when takes occurred were also noted.

It confirmed my suspicions that by far the most important factor in pike fly fishing is the water temperature.

Pike are poikilothermic – organisms whose internal temperature fluctuates as a consequence of variation in the ambient environmental temperature. Their metabolism favours them lying still and ambushing prey as they pass nearby. They do not use their metabolisms to heat or cool themselves. They are at the whim of the elements.

Chasing prey has a high energy cost and obviously this is not the preferred option for the pike when the governing water temperature is low. However, if the water temperature is conducive to replacing energy easily, they will be happy to move in search of prey. I call this the Optimal Temperature Zone (OTZ). Outside of the zone, the fish will lessen their hunting activity.

The OTZ varies depending on how far north or south you are. For Scotland and Northern Ireland it is between 11°C and 15°C. For much of England, Wales and Southern Ireland it is between 12°C and 16°C, according to my records.

## VERNAL EQUINOX

An equinox is when the length of daylight matches that of night. There are two in the year. The vernal equinox occurs in late March, and after that point we start getting longer days and lifting temperatures due to the balance shifting in favour of sunlight. April is usually when the pike fishing proper gets underway. In the cold spring of 2013, however, the temperatures struggled to rise. In the UK it was the coldest for many decades. In real terms it was 2°C colder than the seasonal norm and all the plants and natural events were two weeks behind.

In the past three years this pattern seems to be the norm and the downside is that the slow progression of winter to spring and spring to summer is now being compressed. We now have a shorter spring, where temperatures go from freezing to hot in a much shorter space of time.

A recent experience illustrates my point. The weather websites were predicting a sharp rise in temperature for the first time this spring, which was what we were waiting for, so a friend and I decided to have a few days going after pike.

The first day was warm enough at 12°C. We positioned the boat and I slid the thermometer over the side. The water temperature was 9.5°C. I was slightly disappointed, bearing in mind the growing air temperature. To cut a long story short, we blanked.

## MONSTER PIKE

The next day started sunny with an incredible air temperature of 17°C. It was another cracking day and we headed back to the bays we had fished the day before. The thermometer, when removed from the water, showed 12°C.

We fished hard on the first drift and I hooked a spirited jack of around 5lb. I was pleased to get the take, but I don't like hitting jacks at this time of year as it can often mean a day of small fish and nothing bigger.

We fished on and decided to head ashore for lunch. As we did, a bank of cloud rolled in and we saw a further hike in temperatures of 1°C. The afternoon water temperature was now 13°C and we had a lovely covering of cloud – perfect!

We were chatting away as we drifted between an island and the shore when, as

Big fish need a big mouthful! Don't skimp on fly size and don't forget those wire leaders!

"As I retrieved, my line locked up solid. This pike had taken my fly and just kept moving forward as if nothing had happened."

I retrieved, my line locked up solid. This pike had taken my fly and just kept moving forward as if nothing had happened. Line disappeared from my reel at a steady, relentless pace. No jumping, no thrashing, just steady, determined forward motion.

I now had two hands on the rod and cranked up the drag on the reel, but it just kept on keepin' on! I watched the ever-lengthening backing slide out into the loch.

After a battle of about half an hour, we finally got a sight of the fish – it was colossal. When we eventually got most of her bulk into the net we were astounded by how broad she was – without doubt the broadest pike I

If the water temperature is conducive to the pike replacing energy, it's time to go hunting!

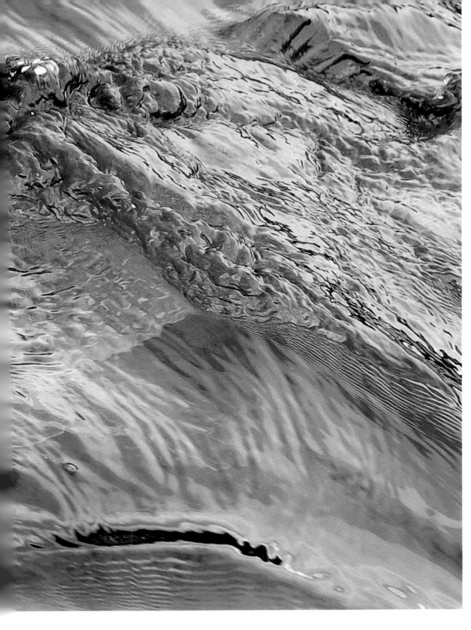

Andy with a good fish taken from a shallow bay, an area where the water temperature can rise fast.

have ever seen. The raw power of this 35lb fish was incredible and after unhooking it I was delighted to see that big tail slowly and purposefully take her back into the depths as my hand parted company with the wrist of her tail.

A common factor had come into play: the first big warm-up of the season. My pre-spawning pike had reacted to nature's sign that spring had suddenly arrived and she was now actively hunting.

Once the post-spawning period has finished, the pike's feeding becomes a more measured and sedate affair. As water temperatures increase, most of the bigger pike hang around the deeps to avoid the warm shallows.

In mid to late summer when the water temperature reaches its highest point, larger pike will resort to hunting at dusk or dawn. Dawn is the first light to illuminate the nocturnally cooled water and an excellent time to be an ambush hunter, considering the low visibility and favourable temperatures.

The ascent of the sun not only brings light, but warmth as well that reheats the water. Pike can lose interest in hunting and indeed feeding when the water temperature gets too high.

## AUTUMNAL EQUINOX

It will often be the case that when the pike are taking static natural baits, like a dead roach for example, they will not take a fly. A memorable example springs to mind.

I was fishing a large loch popular with pike anglers of all persuasions. The weather up until that point had been benign and mellow for early October. As I passed the small flotilla of craft I asked each anchored-up deadbaiter how the sport was. "Nothing" was the usual response.

I started my initial drift and the first cast produced a tidy 10-pounder. Soon enough over went the rod again, an eight-pounder. The reel screamed a while later as I hooked a 15-pounder! In total I landed 16 pike, yet all the other boats in the bay recorded a blank.

The next morning I couldn't wait to get back into the boat, this time joined by one of my regular boat partners. I worriedly brushed the frost from the gunwales of the boat as we headed back to the bay. The lads with the legered deadbaits were having a ball, in fact they had a steady series of runs all day. The entire bay resounded to the sound of electronic bleepers going off.

We, however, caught no fish to the fly, not even a tweak, not even a follow. The

# "If low water temperatures stay steady for a few days then suddenly rise, pike will come on the feed and sport can be good."

This colossal 35lb fish was taken in an afternoon with cloud cover and when the water temperature rose by only 1°C, proof indeed of catching in the OZT!

reason? The night before saw temperatures plummet. There had been an overnight frost and the water temperature had dropped by 3°C. In the world of the poikilothermic, that's huge. Crashing temperatures lead to energy conservation. They had to choose how they would feed that day, chase or not chase. They chose smell over sight.

## THE BIG FREEZE

Pike will feed through the colder months in very low water temperatures and even under ice. They put their metabolism on idle, eating less and decreasing their activity. When they feed they will generally do so during the warmest part of the day, often not feeding for days on end if they have had a decent-sized meal.

The greatest exception to the OTZ rule is if low water temperatures stay steady for a few days then suddenly rise, in which case pike will come on the feed and sport can be good until it falls again.

A frost will kill the activity stone dead.

During winter the water generally struggles to heat up and this is why deadbaiting is so popular at this time – smell over sight.

However, a caveat to all these theories is "Landing your fly on the nose of the pike". If a bar of chocolate falls into your lap, do you refuse it? Of course not, and neither will pike refuse a fly, no matter what the temperature.

After recording water and air temperatures over the years, I'm struck by how often the water temperature is very close to that of the air temperature.

The lesson to be learnt is that the air temperature drives everything. It can save a fishing day by raising the water temperature or spoil it by cooling the water, so whenever you head out after pike, keep an eye on the temperature!

## ANGLER FILE ANDY BOWMAN

A wild-trout and salmon flyfisher since early childhood, Andy Bowman has travelled widely in search of many species including salmon, sailfish and pike. Conceptual fly design and fishing in wild places is a passion that endures.

George Barron looks at the new kid on the block, the Muddler, and how it has increased the catch rate of many UK and Irish anglers.

# CAUSE A COMMOTION

Prior to pulling the cork on a half-decent bottle of rioja and settling down to begin writing this feature about Muddler patterns for wild brown trout, I decided to check out the patterns, theories and musings of those three illustrious authors and anglers, Messrs Headley, O'Reilly and Morgan, whose books, respectively Trout & Salmon Flies of Scotland, Ireland and Wales, are a serious source of reference for anglers the world over.

The books were all written around 15 years ago – a long time in fishing terms – but certainly time enough for them to recognise the effectiveness of the Muddler since it was first devised by Don Gapen for fishing in Ontario in 1953 and introduced into the UK during the 1960s by Nottingham tackle dealer Tom Saville.

Strangely, Peter O'Reilly makes no reference to Muddlers in any form but Moc Morgan credited us a few examples tied in bigger hook sizes, giving reference to sea trout and salmon dressings.

Stan Headley, meanwhile, introduced the Muddler theme upwards of six times in his book; definitely a fisherman after my own heart when it comes to the pursuit and catching of wild brown trout. God bless his cotton socks.

Before they came along we had Bumbles and the like doing a similar job. However, Muddlers were likely the first type of wet fly to be classified as a real disturbance pattern. Albeit innocently, we possibly didn't fully realise the effect that they created when pulled at speed, as was the fashion during those years.

The present day reservoir style of ripping Boobies on a floating line with a couple of imitative nymphs down the cast, then slowing to a figure-of-eight retrieve, is not too far removed in technique from using a mini-Muddler top dropper, fished loch-style with a couple of imitative wet flies behind.

It would appear that disturbance is the name of the game when it comes to stirring trout.

From memory, early commercial Muddler dressings weren't the prettiest of things. Most were very basic and normally tied big using deer hair so thick and bulky you could surely clean the chimney with them.

Then it changed a bit. Small became the new game in town; mini-Muddlers in size 12 and even smaller were the order of the day, often preferably tied as a little double to fish on the point. No self-respecting conventional wet fly or lure was safe from deer hair during the 1980s and 1990s because we shoved a Muddler head on anything that caught trout in its wet-fly state.

The numerous Muddler patterns that we banged out then had a fairly good track record when it came to thinning out rainbows around the major stillwaters. However, undoubtedly, they always seemed to create far more interest when wild brown trout were the quarry. This is likely because brownies in their natural environment are far more territorial and aggressive creatures, certainly at the tail end of the season when the notion turns to spawning.

The first three notable Muddler patterns to enter my fly box were the bog-standard Gold version, the Soldier Palmer and the Green Peter. During the early 1980s when, in my humble opinion, Chew Valley was the best top-of-the-water fishery in the UK, its rainbow and brown trout fell in love with Gold Muddlers – bow waving behind a stripped floating-line retrieve, the cast being made up of a Muddler on the point, Silver Invicta on the middle dropper and, wait for it, a Tandem Worm Fly on the top dropper. When was the last time a Tandem Worm Fly slid across the Roman Shallows?

I digress slightly as my eyes mist over. The favoured tying of the Gold Muddler at that time, certainly among my group of fishing buddies, was the version tied on a size 12 Partridge Outpoint Double – sadly these irons are no longer made. I can't really explain why we preferred doubles. Possibly they helped the Muddler dig in a little deeper to help anchor the cast and stop it skating because of the rate of knots we pulled them back. Muddlers have sort of gone out of fashion a bit these last few years but I still give them a swim on a regular basis. When the trout have seen lots of the same stuff day after day, something slightly different, like a Muddler, might just turn it around and get you some interest. They seem to perform best as biggish wave flies or, alternatively, in small sizes they're handy enough around the edge of a ripple over feeding fish.

I'm moving now from the old to the new. New venues are always exciting to visit in terms of preparing a fresh box of flies to tackle a situation where you've only been privy to someone else's local knowledge, or what you have managed to glean from previous articles and books written about the place. On most international matches that I was involved in, I'd stretch to a new fly box and fill it with fresh versions of the advised menu, or variations on the theme of my own interpretation.

Prior to the 2011 Spring International I'd heard so much about the quality of fishing on the Loch of Harray on Orkney, and the totally diverse selection of flies required, that I got a bit carried away at the vice. It was no secret that Harray trout liked Muddlers. Nothing like any of the Muddlers that I had ever tied or used before but, as it transpired, we found a couple of things to fool a few trout.

> "When the trout have seen the same stuff day after day, something different, like a Muddler, might just get you some interest."

The following two dressings are nothing revolutionary but they did royally for me, fished on a medium sinker among those daphnia-feeding, yellow-finned, beautiful Harray trout. It's a 1,200-mile round trip from my house but I'd love to return one day.

I don't have names for these two Muddlers. I think one is a close copy of what's known as the Merkister Maid and the other I simply refer to as the Black & Silver Muddler.

If they are conventionally known as something else, I apologise. White-headed flies and Orkney peach seem to figure in a number of flies from Harray and these two were very effective.

## BLACK & SILVER MUDDLER

**Hook:** Fulling Mill Competition, sizes 10 and 12
**Tail:** A few strands of peach feather fibre
**Rib:** Silver wire
**Body:** Silver tinsel
**Wing:** Black mink strip
**Head:** White deer hair

## MERKISTER MAID

**Hook:** Fulling Mill Competition, sizes 10 and 12
**Tail:** A pinch of sunburst marabou **Rib:** Silver wire
**Body:** Pearly holo over black thread
**Wing:** Three parts – first black marabou, second sunburst marabou and finally a few strands of gold Flashabou.
**Head:** White deer hair

## GOLDEN OLIVE MUDDLER DABBLER

The two other obvious colours for Muddlers when brownies are the target are olive and claret. Olive-dyed deer hair is fairly easy to access but I often struggle to get claret in anything other than the heavy quality. Much of it comes in from America pre-dyed, a land where they recognise olive but don't have a clue about claret — it normally hits our shores purple.

Rather than chase after sub-standard dyed deer hair, I find it easier to use the natural and push the required or desired colour into the fly with good-quality dyed hen hackle run down the length as a body hackle. This works particularly well when incorporated into Dabbler patterns with a Muddler head.

The first Dabbler Muddlers I ever saw were being used by Niall Cromie of the Dromore Angling Club in Ireland. He swore by them on Lough Erne and that great pulling water, Lough Melvin.

The Claret Muddler Dabbler is tied exactly as the golden olive, obviously with a claret seal's fur body and a claret hen body hackle. One bunch of deer hair is adequate because the bronze mallard wing does the job that the first bunch did on the previous dressings.

I've found on recent visits to the west of Ireland, that the wild trout seem to have taken a bit of a fancy to Muddlers and Dabblers that incorporate 1mm to 5mm UV Fritz in the body. That said, I would qualify that by saying these are waters that are darker and peatier to the eye — Lough Mask and suchlike.

**Hook:** Fulling Mill Competition, sizes 10 and 12
**Tail:** Bunch natural pheasant tail
**Rib:** TC wire, hot yellow, small
**Body:** Golden olive seal's fur
**Hackle:** Three turns golden olive hen
**Wing:** Cloaked bronze mallard
**Head:** One bunch of clipped deer hair

## KATE McLAREN MUDDLER

If I were forced to use only one fly to fish for wild brown trout from opening day until the last knockings at the season's end, it would be the Kate McLaren. From John O'Groats to Land's End and every lough I've thrashed in Ireland, this fly has had her name on the score sheet many times. As a wet fly I dress it in many guises, simply tweaking a tail, a tag, or a hackle colour to provide a change from the highly effective traditional pattern. I have no hesitation in stating that a colour mix of black, red and silver, certainly in spring and autumn, is the most effective combination to fool a brown trout. Sticking a Muddler head on the Kate seems almost as natural as putting one foot in front of the other when walking. All the variations work for me but, for whatever reason, I find that Welsh brownies prefer a red tail with a silver butt under to the more conventional yellow toppings.

The dressing can also be jazzed up a wee bit by using different-colour body hackles; red, badger or golden olive being the obvious choices.

**Hook:** Fulling Mill Competition, sizes 10 and 12
**Butt:** Silver tinsel
**Tail:** Dyed red tippets, or natural toppings
**Rib:** Silver wire
**Body:** Black seal's fur hackle: palmered black hen, or try badger, red or golden olive
**Head:** Elk or roe deer

## GOLD MUDDLER (original)

The tail and wing material used on the original Sculpin Minnow Muddler was oak turkey quill, quite pricey and not so easy to acquire. I think brownies are just as happy with hen pheasant secondary. As for deer hair, I prefer elk or roe deer hair, certainly on the size of Muddlers that I tie because they're smaller fibred, softer and tie in much tidier than conventional deer hair, which is too thick and bulky. I also use a fair bit of coastal deer. It bleaches well and lends itself to dying in softer colours, such as various shades of olive.

**Hook:** Fulling Mill Competition, sizes 12 and 10
**Tail and wing:** Folded slip of hen pheasant secondary
**Rib:** Gold wire
**Body:** Gold tinsel
**Head:** Two bunches of deer hair. First bunch tied in more like a wing and not spun. The second, a bigger bunch and spun.

# FULLINGMILL
## RAISING THE GAME

# FLIES FOR ALL SEASONS

**Fulling** Mill is continuously bringing out new, cutting-edge patterns that will keep you catching, every season, the whole year through.

**W**hether you're targeting trout in small streams or hunting specimen fish in the salt, with over 2,000 flies to choose from, Fulling Mill has it covered.

Here we highlight a handful of the company's bestsellers...

## SPRING

**SALMON:** The Kinermony Killer is a new fly, originating on the Spey but has quickly gained a reputation for catching salmon everywhere! The tube version is a superb choice, as it will get down quickly and fish straightaway in high water.

**TROUT:** The KJ Fenton Cat Booby is a standout pattern in spring. If you're keen to get on the banks of those reservoirs 'early doors' then this one is for you – go deep and slow for the best results.

**DESTINATION SALTWATER:** The Sand Prawn has been doing the damage on many of the world's finest flats; it seems that the bonefish can't help themselves and this is a 'must' when you're targeting them.

## SUMMER

**SALMON:** The Cascade, dependable and effective, is a proven salmon fly that you should never be without when summer fishing; the colours make it 'glow' in the water, often enticing reluctant fish to take.

**TROUT:** The KJ Olive Emerger will be effective right from the word go when olives are up and hatching; then, this must the first choice dry for the end of your tippet, ideal in the summer months.

The Mohican May is the best-selling Mayfly pattern and no wonder; it looks just like the real deal and, more importantly, the trout think so too.

## AUTUMN

**SALMON:** The Willie Gunn Skullhead is an increasingly popular choice for the back end; the colours suit that time of year perfectly. The fly is aerodynamically shaped and easy to cast, just the ticket when you're on the water all day long.

**TROUT:** The Rob's Wrapped Minkie will be the last thing that many big trout see, as they can't help but fall for it. This fly is a deadly pattern when the larger fish start fry feeding in earnest.

**PIKE:** The Dougie's Perch has all the key attributes to imitate the fish that most pike are feeding on. Big pike are out to get some weight on before the rigours of winter and spawning so they want a mouthful... this fly delivers.

## WINTER

**GRAYLING:** The Rubber Grub has that lovely segmented look about it, similar to most river nymphs – ideal when you're after grayling. Its weight gets it down to the riverbed and into the grayling's line of sight fast... perfect!

**GRAYLING:** The F-Fly Pinkie may well be small but it's all the more effective for it. This tiny morsel is often enough to bring grayling up when there's a hatch on even the coldest of winter days. Don't leave home without it.

**TROUT:** The Crystal Black Cat has the two colours that we most associate with winter stillwater fishing, that deadly black and green combo. This fly has movement and profile, two essentials for cold water.

Total FlyFisher editor Steve Cullen reveals the secrets
to help you catch a 'double' as autumn turns to winter!

# THINK BIG

Fishing big flies, deep down and into the wind, will see you among the better fish – this huge brown trout was taken yards from the bank.

Speaking for myself, I have always been fixated on big fish. As with most things in life, size is relative – a 1lb brown trout from a small brook is a good one, similarly a grayling weighing a couple of pounds from any river is a fish that we'd all like to catch.

However, I think that for most of us it's in the stillwater arena that big fish – rainbows and brown trout – capture the angler's imagination.

Unlike their smaller counterparts, these fish seem aloof, often behaving in a completely different manner.

The way they behave dictates the tactics we must use in order to catch them. These big trout tend to hold deeper in the water and are often far slower than their smaller brethren. Being big they also need a far larger mouthful in order to make 'chasing' anything worth their while.

To catch these fish then, with any kind of regularity, you must fish deep, retrieve slowly and use a BIG fly!

## TACKLE CHOICE

Most of your normal tackle will do just fine for targeting these big fish, so you can make do with what you've got. I like to tailor my tackle, though, and when I'm after big fish I tend to step things up a gear.

Normally, I will happily target most stillwaters with a lightweight outfit; after all, most of the trout I'll be catching are between 2lb and 5lb, so there are no real problems there.

When specifically looking to target the bigger fish that inhabit small waters, though, I'll beef things up. I like to use a powerful 10ft 7-wt rod with a fast tip-action, a rod that is an out-and-out casting tool, and the reasons for this choice are many.

It will allow me to cast a lot further than a soft-actioned rod, so it is ideal when you're looking to cover a lot of water. Big trout will often take refuge just out of casting range of most anglers, but I want to be able to reach them and the stiffer model will also allow you to pull a hook into a fish's mouth at distance. Finally, the more powerful rod puts you in control pretty much straightaway when you do finally hook a big fish. Make sure that the trout doesn't bully you, if it wants to fight dirty then you've the right tool with which to sway the argument.

I like a reel with a decent drag – I may not get to use it too often but I want it there just in case.

I'll also use a fly line that allows me to cast further and when fishing a floater the Snowbee XS is a good choice. For sunk-line work I'm happy with Airflo Forty Plus lines.

There's no point in using heavy-handed tackle and fishing with thin tippets, it'll only lead to disaster. I use a strong, 8lb to 10lb fluorocarbon, depending on the size of flies that I am using.

I'll always fish with a tapered leader, joining it and the tippet together with the help of a blood knot. I like tapered leaders as they aid turnover massively; when you're using large or weighted flies without a tapered leader there's always the likelihood of the flies kicking left or right. Worse, on the forward cast the leader can collapse and then it won't turn over the fly at all!

Oh, and make sure that you've a net that can cope – it's no good hunting monsters with a little foldaway pan net, you want a strong pole, stiff rim and some deep mesh!

## PROVEN PATTERNS

I tend to go with that age-old adage of "big flies for big fish" as most of my large trout, both browns and rainbows, have fallen victim to large lures. I've not caught many on the usual small-water lures like Vivas and Cat's Whiskers; more meaty mouthfuls with plenty of fur used in the tyings have done far better for me.

Mink, rabbit and pine squirrel are my favourites, they just have so much movement underwater – they undulate and pulse far more than a lure tied with marabou, or any other

### RODS

Use a powerful rod with a stiff action – you'll cast further and pull the hook home.

### LINES

Forty-plus or distance fly lines will allow you to cover more water than the average angler.

### FLIES

Must be big! Those that look like small fish are the best ones to use when going deep and dirty.

# "The rod slammed over and instantly I knew it was big as the fish powered away, staying deep as it did so."

feather for that matter.

Most lures that are tied with these furs, 'matuka style', work really well and offer a wonderful profile that mimics many small fish.

For the last four years, however, I have been using Snakes.

These are long lures created with nothing more than a bit of rabbit or mink strip, a little fishing braid and two hooks, although there's only one hook point. They are long, sinuous, full of life and really do take some beating. They can be tied in a variety of ways and with many colour combinations too – the possibilities are endless.

For me, though, there are four that stand out – natural, white, black and olive. You can, if you wish, decorate the hook shanks of the flies, adding a hackle or even chain-bead eyes for additional weight, but I have to say that I prefer the minimalist approach.

## RED-LETTER DAY

Roxholme Fly Fishery lies in the village of Carlton, in Nottinghamshire, and has only been open a few years, yet it still has the appearance of a more mature water. The fishery is landscaped with little hills, made from the soil that was initially excavated, which gives the place a certain character and charm. There a few little bays and interesting characteristics, like inlets and aerators, all of which will hold fish.

The other good thing with this water is that it is home to some good trout, I dare say a higher percentage than most small waters, but, as

with all fish you've still got to catch them. And with most of the big fish having been caught before, this can be tricky!

Talking to owner Andy MacDonald I found that there had been several good browns coming out of late, most of which had come from deep water – the fishery has depths to 18 feet – so it was with these particular fish in mind that saw me start out on a Forty Plus Di5 line, 15ft leader, a 10lb bonefish tapered leader with five feet of 8lb fluorocarbon and a single white Snake!

My friend, who had joined me for the day, set up with a bung with a buzzer, as well as an Egg setup to fish below it. He thought that most fish would be high in the water.

It was cold, very cold, with a brisk northerly wind blowing in toward the fishing lodge on the south side of the venue. Given my years of accumulated knowledge of fishing on these small venues I knew that this would be the most likely side to encounter the big fish.

The wind creates an undertow, pushing any food out from the banks and into open water. The hope was that any larger trout would be sitting headfirst in the current, down near the bottom, waiting for any food items to come their way.

Now although this water is small, I much prefer the Forty Plus to a normal fly line, for reasons I've already highlighted. Starting at the first platform near the lodge I cast as far as possible, keeping my retrieve slow with a figure-of-eight interspersed with a few 1ft pulls – a default method when after large fish.

The majority of big fish will be deep, and on the downwind shore they will also be facing into your bank. Bear this in mind when fishing your flies.

Wind direction

10 feet

For the first 20 minutes or so I cast and retrieved but only managed one take. My mate, on the other hand, put two 3lb rainbows in the net, both taken on the Egg, six feet deep.

After some recent heavy rain, the water was rather coloured, so I swapped over to a black Snake, my thinking being that the silhouette would stand out better in the murky water.

Halfway through my retrieve, just as the head of the line came in the tip ring, the rod slammed over! Instantly, I knew it was big. I could feel the slow, steady judder of the rod as the fish powered away, staying deep as it did so. Quickly, I put my loose line on to the reel so that I could play the fish off my drag. This is a great way of tiring them faster and you're far more in control should the fish surge away at the last second, which can and does happen!

Slowly, I inched the reel handle round, gaining line each time, bringing the fish closer to my bank and the water's surface. After a hectic tug of war lasting around 10 minutes it came to the top, splashed a few times and gave up, ready for the net!

My first fish of the session and what a trout, it was a huge brown and tipped the scales at a very impressive 10lb 3oz after Andy weighed it for me. Job done, feature in the bag!

Wow, what an amazing start, I didn't think that it could get any better... but it certainly did. On that freezing cold and miserable day, horrible by anybody's standards, I was in seventh heaven!

Fishing my way around the whole south side of the fishery I managed to land another double – a rainbow weighing 13lb 2oz – and five other trout, mostly browns in excess of 8lb. I'll struggle to emulate that ever again!

Yet the chap I was fishing with, who caught more fish than I did, by far, only managed the one trout over 5lb. The other anglers who were there that day struggled to find any big fish too, with only one other double-figure fish that came out between four of them.

## TYING THE SNAKE

**Hook:** Rear – Mini Manta, size 8; front – any large wet-fly hook
**Thread:** White
**Braid:** 15lb sinking
**Wing:** Rabbit or mink
**Body:** Optional, Lite Brite, white

**1** Tie the braid on to the rear hook, using a tucked blood knot.

**2** Place the other hook in the vice, and bring the braid up through the eye, wind it over itself and cover in tying thread. Add glue if you wish.

**3** Place the rear hook back in the vice, add the tying thread and tie in the rabbit at the rear and behind the hook eye. lace in.

**4** Using wire cutters, snip the front hook at the start of the bend. (Placing the barb in foam will prevent bits of metal flying about.)

**5** Replace the front hook in the vice, attach the rabbit at the rear, wind on a body…

**6** … bring the rabbit wing up and over, tie in at head. Tidy up, tie off and add varnish.

A huge male brown trout that tipped the scales at a whopping 10lb 3oz, taken in deep water on a large Snake.

One of them came over to ask what I was doing but he didn't have the flies or the line, so I gave him mine. He landed his best-ever brown trout on his fifth cast, Andy weighed it at just short of 9lb, then took some photos before it was released. The chap then told me that he was forever in my debt, and would I sell him some Snakes!

I dare say that luck played a large part in my success that day, but the way I was fishing – deep, slow, and with very big flies – gave me an edge.

I'm convinced that all three combined, plus the fact that I was the only one brave enough to face into the wind, helped me to contact the water's larger residents.

This technique of fishing 'deep and dirty' has been good to me in the past and it's worked just as well since my day at Roxholme Fly Fishery.

You may not catch as many trout by fishing this way but if you want to sort out the bigger and better fish that lurk in your stillwater, then it has to be the way to go!

## THE MOFFAT MONSTER

There are, of course, a few exceptions to the deep and dirty rule...

I remember well, decades ago, visiting the very popular Moffat Trout Fishery – recently reopened as the Green Frog – virtually every weekend; the fishery was like an aquarium as everything was in it – salmon, brook, golden, brown and rainbow trout, there was even talk of grayling in the place!

The thing was the water was gin clear, thanks to being spring fed, and was one of the few places in Scotland where you could actually stalk fish.

Shaun Ottewell, the owner, had a few 'pets' in the place, some very large trout that always seemed to evade capture. One of these was a very large male brown trout with a big kype on his lower jaw. This huge fish was often to be found sitting at a little inlet, midwater, fins wafting from side to side, looking more or less comatose.

Any angler coming into the fishery would pass the inlet and, as you can imagine, none could pass up the opportunity to have a try for him. You'd see them casting, changing flies and casting again and so on until either a) they got fed up or b) the big brown would swim away, out into open water.

For nearly a year this fish stayed at large, practically uncatchable, until the fateful day it was caught. I was there. It was during a prolific hatch of pond olives that the huge fish succumbed to an angler's fly, one of the Moffat locals. Get this, it took a size 18 Pheasant Tail Nymph fished on the end of 5lb Drennan Double Strength tippet! It was a very, very clever fish!

Despite all those meaty mouthfuls wafting past its face for months on end it never succumbed, but in the end it fell for a fly no bigger than a grain of rice! It weighed 16lb 4oz.

"Just when I thought it couldn't get much better, it did! I landed another double – this time a 13lb-plus rainbow – again taken deep and slow!"

# YELLOW OWL CDC

**This** little pattern has been on the go for a long time as a wet fly. The CDC version, shown here, is becoming increasingly popular now, representing many insects such as buzzers and sedges.

**Hook:** To suit, standard dry or B110, size 10 or 12
**Thread and body:** Light Cahill
**Rib:** Black floss
**Thorax:** Squirrel or rabbit
**Wing:** Five or six CDC feathers
**Wings:** Grizzle hackle tips

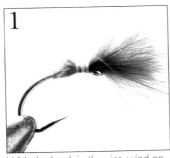

**1** With the hook in the vice, wind on tying thread, then catch in the CDC, tips forward, about the same length as the body. Trim the waste.

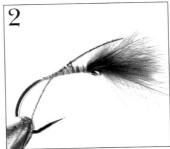

**2** Tidy up the stub ends of CDC with thread wraps. At the back end of the CDC, catch in a 6in length of black floss.

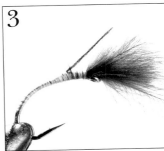

**3** Create a body with several layers of the tying thread, stopping at the thorax area.

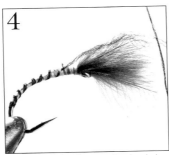

**4** Now wind the floss up the body in nice open turns, again stopping at the thorax.

**5** Trim the waste floss and then create a slim dubbing rope from the squirrel/rabbit fur and wind it up to behind the eye.

**6** Take the tying thread in front of the CDC and finally whip finish before snipping the tying thread. Add varnish if you wish.

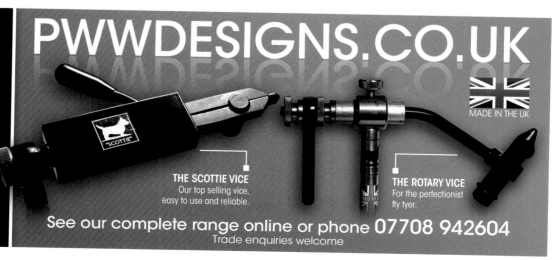

"There's no such thing as bad weather, just bad clothing." The fish thrive in these cold conditions, so get wrapped up, get out there and get catching.

# WINTER

# READY FOR

**England** international Simon Robinson reveals his best-kept secrets to prepare you for the winter fishing ahead.

# ACTION!

**D**uring winter, lure fishing with attractor patterns can be among the most deadly techniques available to the small-stillwater angler. Attractor patterns and lures are considered by many anglers not to involve a great deal of skill and technique.

Nothing could be further from the truth... and during the course of this feature I will aim to show you how you can get the most from your stillwater patterns.

To demonstrate the tactics, I made a visit to Sharpley Springs Fishery in County Durham on a typical early winter day.

Several anglers were already fishing when I arrived and appeared to have little reward to show for their efforts. This is often the case during early morning after a frost. This gave the ideal opportunity to try some of my own lure fishing approaches to tempt these lethargic fish into taking.

When considering how a lure is going to behave in the water, I base my tactics around my choice of line density and the design of the pattern itself. I will now cover both, in turn.

When lure fishing on small stillwaters, I will often place a single nymph on the dropper. This can really prove to be a tremendous addition to your leader, particularly when fishing a ghost tip or floating line. The nymph is often taken on the drop as it descends in a natural manner through the water.

This proved to be the case on my visit to Sharpley Springs, as I hooked two fish at once with only my second cast of the day. In this situation I will net the dropper fish first and land the fish on the point fly by hand – hopefully!

On this occasion it worked and I was rewarded with two nice rainbows in the net. These were quickly followed by several other fish, mainly to the lure patterns, including two tremendously conditioned doubles – truly excellent fishing!

As you can see, I like to carry a good selection of lines when stillwater fishing. These lines all have different applications when spring lure fishing because, when combined with lure patterns of different designs and weights, they can produce a specific depth and action which, on its day, can outfish all others.

I carry my line selection in a reel case, which not only protects my reels from damage in my tackle bag but it also allows easy access to the full range while on the bank; these are my top, all-time lines.

## FLOATING LINE

Many anglers consider that the use of a floating line is restricted to warmer months and the use of imitative patterns. The floating line can, however, be a valuable addition to the lure angler's selection.

Personally, I carry a WF8 floating line when bank fishing and use it for two, main lure fishing applications. Firstly, the floating line can be used with a heavily leaded pattern to create an up-and-down action. This action can be very tempting to winter rainbows, particularly around lunch time when temperatures are at their warmest.

The second application is to use a floating line with a lightly weighted or unweighted pattern. The buoyancy of the floating line holds the fly up in the water and stops the lure from snagging the lake bed. This allows very slow retrieves to be used and, on very cold days when fish are unwilling to chase, this can be critical.

### GHOST TIP

When winter fishing, one of my most successful lines is Cortland Ghost Tip. During winter I choose the 15ft, clear-tip version. This line has a very similar use to the full floating line as it allows the angler to control a very slow retrieve as well as giving the up-and-down motion described above.

The sinking tip has one important difference in that it allows the angler to create these retrieve styles at a greater depth than a full floating line. The sinking tip also has the effect of reducing any bow in the fly line if I'm fishing a crosswind.

### CLEAR INTERMEDIATE

This line is, without doubt, the most versatile line in the lure angler's armoury. It can be used with a full range of lure patterns and, by using the countdown method to locate the taking depth, fish can be followed throughout the day.

It can also be used for a slow retrieve over deep water. I use this line as a starting point on most occasions and depending on the depth, the retrieve and the lure-action preferences of the fish I will then look to change to maximise fishing effectiveness and efficiency.

### TYPE III (MEDIUM SINKER)

This line is a true sinker and I will fish it in two main roles. Firstly, I will use this line when fishing a standard or heavily weighted lure over deep water, in excess of 10 feet in depth. I will often change to this line if I am counting more than 20 seconds for my intermediate line to reach the taking depth.

I prefer to use a faster-sinking line than swapping to a heavier pattern, as fish will often prefer the fly travelling at a level depth. The

second occasion where the type III sinker can be the best line is on those occasions where a fast retrieve is working.

Slower-sinking intermediates tend to rise at a much steeper angle towards the rod tip and can have the effect of pulling a lightweight pattern out of the taking zone.

### TYPE 7 (FAST SINKING)

This line is the fastest sinking of the lines I carry. I will use this line when fish are holding very close to the lake bed and in depths of water in excess of 15 feet. If fish are holding at these depths, then using anything other than a fast sinker will result in a great deal of wasted time.

On days when fish are only feeding for short periods, the angler who is getting the most casts at the correct depth will be the most successful. This line is also very important to

1 Match the fly line to the
depth and action of the fly
and how you wish to present it
to the fish. Think about creating
an undulating motion if the
standard retrieves fail.

2 Use lures of different styles
to suit the retrieve and the
depth the fish are at. Carry
a good selection of weights
and designs to maximise your
chances of catching throughout
the day.

3 Try a drab nymph such as
a Pheasant Tail or Buzzer
on the dropper; this will often
produce several bonus fish
during the day.

Two fish on
at once!

You can do it too; just follow
the principles in this feature.

the booby angler. You can use a buoyant lure to
either present a pattern very slowly close to the
bottom or to create an undulating motion with
a twitch retrieve and longer leader. Both of
these actions can be deadly during winter.

## FLY PATTERNS

As well as the selection of fly lines, I will also
carry a very healthy selection of lures! I have
recently taken a leaf out of my river fishing
box and now carry a selection of my favourite
lures in various weights. As a general rule I will
carry my lures in four weights.

## UNWEIGHTED

These lures are used when the fish require
a very slow retrieve. These are very useful,
particularly on days when fish are holding in
the surface layers. These patterns are dressed
with no weight under the dressing or by
simply using a plastic bead at the head of the
fly.

   The lightly weighted lures can be fished very
slowly at any depth, and depending on your
choice of fly line will hold at a specific depth.
During winter, fish will often be very reluctant
to follow a pattern that changes depth.

   A pattern fishing on a level plain will
often be taken when a pattern changing
depth constantly will only result in
follows. Unweighted lures do have a slight
disadvantage in that they are difficult to cast
into a headwind due to the fact that they are
relatively large and lightweight.

   Shortening the length of your leader and
reducing the amount of line that you attempt
to shoot on the forward cast can reduce this
problem.

## LIGHTWEIGHT

These lures are weighted to give the pattern

sinking depth and action. If I am looking
to give the pattern an undulating motion,
particularly for use with a floating or ghost
tip line, I will weight the pattern with the bulk
of the weight, in the form of fine lead wire,
towards the head of the pattern.

   I also carry a selection of lures that are
lightly weighted with a bead at the head.
This simply takes away the need to lead the
underbody. In addition, it offers an excellent
opportunity to use the range of coloured
and metallic beads currently available to the
modern fly dresser.

   The bright-green beads currently available
perfectly complement deadly Cat's Whisker
and Black Tadpole patterns.

## HEAVYWEIGHT LURES

These patterns certainly carry a lot of weight!
I will tie these patterns with tungsten beads or
up to 40 turns of lead wire under the dressing.
These patterns are carried to achieve great
depth when fishing straight into deep water
or when casting into a very strong headwind.
The lures can also be fished on a full range
of sinking lines, when the fish are showing
a definite preference for a pattern with an
exaggerated motion through the water. These
patterns, due to their heavy weight, really
do rise and fall in the water on a stop-start
retrieve and exaggerate the movement of the
lightweight lures.

## BUOYANT LURES

Finally, I carry a selection of buoyant lures in
the form of Booby and Razzler patterns. These
are again carried in a range of colours and
sizes. These patterns are very versatile and I do
not intend to go into great detail about them
as several articles have already been published
regarding their use.

Reliable fluorocarbon is a vital part of the armoury…

… especially when the trout are this big!

As far as the winter angler is concerned they simply cannot be ignored. They are best fished on a type III or type 7 sinker at this time of year. If fish are showing a preference for a slowly retrieved pattern near the lake bed, the booby can give you far more control than any standard lure pattern.

Alternatively, fishing the buoyant pattern on a sinking line with a stop-start retrieve can produce a very exciting action. Please, however, check the fishery rules before using boobies on sinking lines and never fish them static if you intend to release fish – enough said!

## LURE DRESSING STYLES

So far, I have covered the use of lines and weighted lures. The third and final point to consider when it comes to getting ready for action, is the style of the lure that you are going to use. I do carry a wide range of styles and new ones are constantly being created. Here are my top three styles: the ones I would certainly not be without on any winter trip.

## TADPOLES

This is an excellent general lure and can be fished in all weights and colours and on any type of line. Try carrying a good selection of Fritz or Chenille patterns in a range of colours. The marabou tail gives this pattern its action.

This movement is exaggerated by adding weight to the dressing of the fly, either in the form of lead wire or a bead as described earlier. Try using a pattern with flash in the tail if the conditions are bright as this often makes a big difference.

## ZONKERS

These patterns are tied with a strip of rabbit skin along the back. These patterns are best fished on a slow retrieve and as a result I usually tie them with little weight under the dressing. These flies produce a very different movement to the tadpole, which only moves in the tail. Fish these patterns if fish are taking on a very slow retrieve, which can be vital in

winter. These patterns are also very effective at depth as they have a very strong silhouette.

## FLEXI-FLOSS WORMS

This is the most modern of the lure styles I carry. This pattern's movement comes from the long Flexi-Floss legs at either end of the pattern. This pattern is carried in a range of colours also. It is best fished with a stop-start retrieve, as each pause will cause the fly to 'kick'.

It is a pattern that is very effective during winter, particularly if the water is clear. On my visit to Sharpley Springs it was deadly. If you have not tried it yet, you must!

So, next time you are out on the bank, try thinking outside the normal boundaries of fly and line selection. Think about the action of your fly and the ways you can alter and improve it and I am sure that you will be in for lots of action with lots of fish.

## FACT FILE

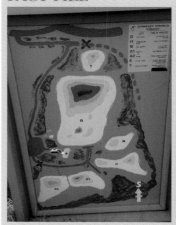

**Venue:** Sharpley Springs
**Make-up:** Five spring-fed lakes with excellent clarity. Fishing is from platforms
**Location:** A quarter of a mile off the B1404 Houghton le Spring to Seaham road which is three minutes from the A19 Seaham Junction and 10 minutes from the A1(M)
**Contact:** Simon Weightman
**Tel:** 0191 5818045
**Mobile:** 07860 757527

A weighted fly accounted for this 10lb-plus fish.

# IT'S ALL ABOUT
# MOBILITY

Craig Barr believes that it doesn't matter how large the water is that you fish, just stay mobile and you'll catch.

The choice of venues available to stillwater trout anglers these days is as broad as it is long. Day-ticket fisheries range from Worcestershire's Broad Oak complex and its two small lakes of one acre and three acres, to mighty Rutland Water and its sprawling 3,300 acres.

Many anglers take one look at the expanse a reservoir such as Rutland covers and are too daunted by the prospects of venturing on to such a vast water.

For anyone wishing to try their hand at taming these bigger venues I feel it's a good idea to first cast a line on what I would call a halfway-house fishery. These are venues that are large enough to give you a taste of what tackle and tactics are needed before taking on the 'big boys'.

Elinor Trout Fishery, near Thrapston in Northamptonshire, is one of these venues when it comes to size. Visitors are faced with 50 acres of spring-fed gin-clear limestone water, which, thanks to the alkaline content, has an abundance of natural food making the trout grow fat and fit.

It is the perfect setting, the ideal stepping stone to larger waters. Once you have the confidence to cope with a fishery of this size making the next move will seem easy. I always tell myself a trout is a trout, which just needs catching wherever it swims. If anything, I believe that the bigger the water, the easier the trout can be to catch. It can be like a game of cat and mouse. On small waters they can become more elusive, but with a little lateral thinking you should be able to work out where the trout should or could be.

This can be done by looking for features in the water, points and promontories, dam walls, weed beds, deep holes, and the like.

I have fished some small waters where people almost know the trout by name as they have been in there for so long and caught so often.

These fish have seen every fly imaginable and become almost impossible to catch, so you really need to make every cast count. However, one of the most important aspects of fly fishing, no matter what the size of water, is to stay on the move.

During my visit I ditched the 8-wt rod I would normally use on reservoirs and opted for my 6/7-wt rod. Distance casting isn't always needed on this size of lake – in my opinion, presentation becomes more

important on smaller lakes. With regular fishing activity the trout can become smarter a whole lot quicker, compared to those on large reservoirs.

Before I put any flies on my cast I noticed that the grass was full of daddy-longlegs after the recent rains, and with a brisk wind blowing it was a 'no-brainer' that one had to go on my cast.

It turned out to be a wise decision. As I approached the water by the dam, I saw two trout splash no more than three feet from the bank, and judging by the commotion they were certainly hitting the daddies. On closer inspection the inner shoreline was littered with these clumsy-looking insects.

I always like to give the fish a variety of flies to choose from, so opted to fish three flies; a Daddy on the point, a Cruncher on the middle dropper and a size 12 red holographic Diawl Bach on the top dropper. A three-course menu will always look better than a single offering!

This is also more or less what I would do on a large water, as a team works very much in your favour.

Within 30 seconds of my flies hitting the water everything tightened up and I was into a fish. It had to have taken the Daddy, or so I thought. In fact, it had taken the Cruncher. It was soon netted but not a big one, about 1½lb. I just can't seem to connect with anything big at the moment!

With plenty of other trout continuing to move close in I presented my flies time and time again, thinking that I would emulate my instant success. Sadly, to no avail.

## MOVE ON

After several swirls, and a couple of plucks at the flies I knew it was time to move on because these trout were simply not playing ball.

I have found that it's often better to move on and try to find a taking fish rather than waste precious time trying to coax an unwilling specimen on to the hook.

Fishery manager Ed Foster had advised me that the top left-hand corner of the lake was producing a good number of fish. Sadly for me, though, he'd also told plenty of other anglers, and when I reached the spot a handful of locals were already in position with a stack of fish rising right in front of them.

I positioned myself 20 feet to the left of the last angler and, with great expectation, cast out my line.

The water in front of me was deep enough to hold fish so there was no need to wade as a bank of nearside weed, and the food secreted within, was bound to attract them.

## CLUELESS

I have to say it is not often that I am stumped when fishing, but for the first time in many years I was left scratching my head as my two neighbours caught fish after fish. I had one pull in an hour! And they were using plain Crunchers and Diawl Bachs too!

Frustration was getting the better of me and it was time for another move.

I found a sheltered corner of the lake, and as I settled in I saw several fish move on the surface.

Looking through my fly box I opted for a Big Red, an old faithful dry fly and

"Within 30 seconds of my flies hitting the water everything tightened up and I was into a fish."

A wonderfully marked little brown trout taken from the productive top end of the fishery.

This lively trout actually took a liking to a Cruncher – so much for intuition!

**1** Inspect any weed in the margins for food forms.

**2** This inspection revealed some shrimps and hoglice.

**3** A floater, an intermediate and a sinking line will cover all the depths.

**4** Use a powerful rod for lures and a lighter outfit for nymphs and dries.

**5** Surface patterns, whether Boobies or dry flies, catch the trout's attention.

a real reservoir favourite that works equally as well on small waters. I attached a new leader, of 6lb breaking strain rather than the 8lb I'd started with, and now fished the single fly as the shallow water dictated, to minimise disturbance and allow me very accurate presentation.

The change of tactics brought a brief bit of interest when I lifted into a reasonably good-sized rainbow, only for it to quickly throw the hook!

With still only one fish to show for my efforts the question that was bugging me was: where was I going wrong?

It was obvious the fish were very high in the water, as I would often see a dorsal fin break the surface as a trout cruised just underneath.

## A HARD DOSE OF REALITY

As I've said, fishing on small waters can be tricky and these fish were no fools; in fact they were very smart. They'd ignored everything I'd thrown at them! I took some time out to gather my thoughts and try and figure out what to do next.

Then the anglers I'd watched catching all those fish earlier packed their stuff away and walked by me.

I chatted to two of them and discovered they'd taken a staggering 28 fish between them! Either they were doing something extraordinary or they just happened to be in exactly the right spot at the right time!

The moment of truth was about to be revealed as I moved on to the area they had occupied all morning.

## FAST AND FURIOUS ACTION

As I stood in the hotspot it became amazingly apparent that the trout seemed to be literally within an area of 10 square metres. I laid my rod down and just sat there, mesmerised.

During my 10-minute break sitting on the bank and surveying the water, I counted 19 rises all within this remarkably small area.

It was truly incredible how many fish were in this small part of the lake. Whatever was holding them here had kept them there all day. I had been fishing just yards to the right of

these fish earlier and yet only managed one pull in an hour – incredible!

We all have our favourite fly, and I am no different. The Blue-Flash Damsel is my banker and after tying it on I vowed that if it failed, then I would head home with my tail between my legs.

Well, I only went and caught five fish in five casts! Too good to be true? Not really, as I then switched to a Sunken Daddy and my catch rate continued at the same unprecedented rate!

To be honest, I don't think it would have mattered what was on the end, I'm sure I would have caught on it in that spot. I could have continued, but what was the point? It's never that good when you catch all the time.

### HOLDING AREA

So what had I done right or, more importantly, what had I been doing wrong?

In this particular instance a weed bed, a big one at that, which must have held a huge bounty of food was clearly visible 15 yards from the bank. This is what was holding a massive shoal of trout in the confined area.

This little episode highlights the need to keep on the move if you're not catching any trout. Smaller waters can be very popular, especially at the weekends, and many times I have seen anglers enjoying hectic sport one minute only for it to stop the next! This is when we start to evaluate why this has happened – is it because the sun has come out, the fish are full or they have gone down?

We have all at some point used any of these reasons for the slowdown in rod-bending action, whereas more often than not, after all the casting and catching, the fish may have simply moved further along the shoreline.

In the early days of fly fishing anglers were armed with a rod, a shoulder bag and a pair of thigh waders, so they could easily keep on the move when one area failed to produce. Nowadays we seem to go with everything but the kitchen sink, making it more difficult to up sticks and move once all your gear is laid out on the bank.

The key to successful sport on medium to large waters is to stay on the move!

By moving around the fishery, casting here and there, it wasn't long before Craig hit a hotspot…

"I caught five fish in five casts! Too good to be true? Not really, I then switched to a Sunken Daddy and my catch rate continued.."

… and the action was fast and furious!

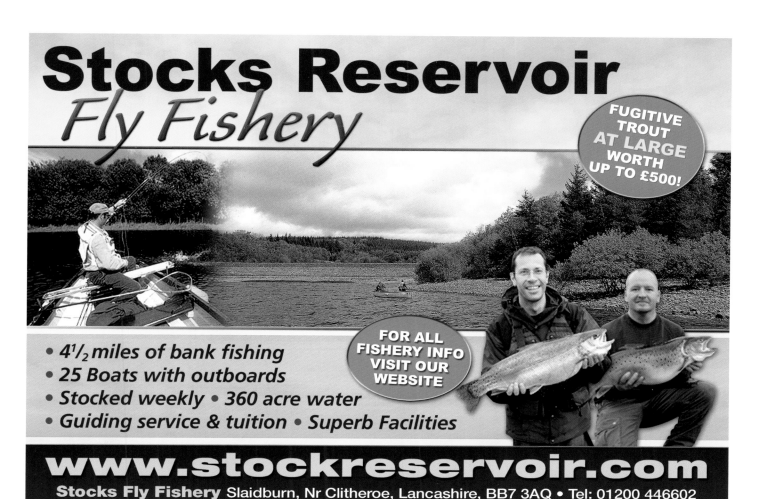

Total FlyFisher is the magazine aimed at fly anglers with an appetite for instruction. Every month it features the latest tips and techniques to give you success in every fly fishing situation.

Featuring some of the UK's highest profile contributors, great interviews, honest tackle reviews and dedicated venue and fly-tying sections, it's the read the modern fly angler shouldn't be without!

**ON SALE** on the second Thursday of every month

**SAVE 10%** **Six issues for only £17.28***

**12 issues for only £30.72*** **SAVE 20%**

*Only available at:*

# dhpsubs.co.uk/totalflyfisher

*or by calling* **0845 345 0253**

*Conditions apply, offers correct at time of going to print. Visit website for details.

# DEFAULT DABBLERS

**George** Barron ties his favourite style of fly – the often-talked about Dabbler, at times a harvester of wild brown trout!

I'm going to tell you a story about a little bit of fishing and fly-tying history, or folklore even, call it what you like.

Not too ancient a story as such, as it only dates back about one fishing generation to around the late 1980s or early 1990s. It's about how the now-iconic Dabbler was invented, created, discovered or just happened to come about by accident... I'll leave you to come to your own conclusion.

It's a story of discovery and excitement that came at a time when change was slow to happen and be universally accepted as something positively 'new' or revolutionary, certainly in the realms of traditional loch-style fishing for wild brown trout from a drifting boat.

Whether you love it or hate it – a wee bit like Marmite really – there is no doubt that competitive fly fishing has driven and been responsible for most of the revolutionary changes to happen in modern fly fishing. Take modern stillwaters and high-density stocking out of the equation and most of us would still be popping down the local river and flicking traditional wets down and across the flow, in pursuit of a rapidly diminishing head of 8in brownies.

## REAL FISH

There are exceptions, though; every angler that can cast a line should slip over that big pond to the west of Wales and have a crack at some real fish, those being the brownies that abide in the great western loughs of Ireland.

At times they don't come too easily to the net, but Irish brown trout are still the number-one choice of trout for the dinner plate, or to put a serious bend in a rod and be returned to the water to fight another day. These wild, indigenous fish bear absolutely no resemblance to, or perform like, the stocked hybrid browns that are so often raved about and often show up

on the catch returns throughout the major UK stillwaters.

But I digress slightly, what I'm really going to tell you about is a fly that revolutionised trout fishing for Ireland's wild trout and, to some extent, has also breathed new life and generated a fresh, albeit traditional, approach to catching trout throughout the UK.

Back in the days before you only had to lash a few wraps of chenille on a hook or create ugly things with foam eyes, chuck them out and pull them back though a few thousand fresh stockies and be back in the lodge before the breakfast dishes were washed, there was a competition called the Benson & Hedges.

To take part your team of six anglers had to be members of the same club, affiliated to the National body of whichever country they were based. This format bred a strong national club base and meant that the number of teams trying to qualify for the international final often had to fish three or even four matches before they got there.

## DROMORE ANGLING CLUB

The strongest team from Ireland at that time was the Dromore Angling Club, who seemed to make it through to the final most years. Its squads at that time included such illustrious names as Bingham, Steele, Cromie and the McClearn brothers among them.

Anyhow, the 'Dabbler' story goes that, while a couple of these lads were practising for an Irish final on Lough Erne (or could have been Melvin) one of them 'found' a pattern that was doing a lot of damage among the wild trout the day before the match. Donald McClearn phoned his team-mate Freddie to get the dressing of the Gosling-looking fly and put together his interpretation as described to him over the telephone. Needless to say, Dromore won the qualifier. The fly became known as the Dabbler

Quality brown trout like this beauty from Ireland's Lough Corrib are catchable when you use Dabblers, just keep them simple!

simply because that was Donald's nickname – Dabbler McClearn – and the rest is history.

The first two Dabblers I ever processed were given to me by Donald, either in 1990 or 1992, when he fished as a member of the Irish Loch Style team on Llyn Brenig. The two flies were tied on size 12 hooks, one was claret and the other was golden olive and they were both fairly sombre-looking patterns. However, their apparent effectiveness was not down to what they looked like, more the way they worked in the water.

## NOT ROCKET SCIENCE

It was explained to me then that what made the Dabbler so successful was the way the bronze mallard wing was tied in to cloak about four-fifths of the body. Not rocket science really, when you consider the fly was designed to be stripped fast across the trout's window to induce a take. The cloaking, if properly done, should create the effect of trapping an air bubble under the wing that somehow bounces light and body colour, creating what can only be described as a very lifelike hatching or distressed morsel that appears to be very attractive to wild trout.

## THE FIRST TWO

Let's take a look at the original two patterns I was given by Donald as they still work as well today as they did when they first burst on to the scene 25 years ago, the Claret Dabbler and the Golden Olive Dabbler.

In the tying, I like to brush up the seal's fur before tying in the wing as I like the haloed effect it creates around the body; it's the same old adage, movement means life. I prefer to use bronze mallard in the medium to smaller sizes in my flies for a couple of reasons, one being that they are a bit lighter in colour and spread so much easier when tying in than the large dark feathers that are more heavily coated in preening oil and are more inclined to gel and stick together. It's techy I know, but I like to collect my Dabbler bronze feathers from the year prior to using them, as I feel they dry off a bit and spread better.

The permutations for the tyer to play around with these two flies are endless – shove a pearly rib on them to jazz them up, simply add an extra head hackle or, as is my favourite 'big wind' tactic, bulk it to create a bit of a disturbance by adding a Muddler head after the mallard wing.

Then again, in light winds as recommended during olive hatches in some parts of the

## SILVER DABBLER REILLY
**Hook:** Fulling Mill Comp, size 10
**Tail:** Natural pheasant tail
**Rib:** Silver wire or stretched pearly
**Body:** Silver tinsel
**Body hackle:** Palmered light red game
**Wing:** Cloaked bronze mallard
**Cheeks:** Natural JC splits
**Head:** Red tying thread

## PETER ROSS DABBLER
**Hook:** Fulling Mill Comp, sizes 10 and 12
**Tail:** Pheasant tail – try red early and late season
**Rib:** Fine silver wire
**Body:** Silver tinsel full length, then front third overdressed with red seal's fur
**Body hackle:** Well-marked badger or black hen
**Wing:** Cloaked bronze mallard
**Cheeks:** Optional – natural JC or dyed red

"The original two patterns I was given still work as well today as they did when they first burst on to the scene 25 years ago."

## GOLDEN OLIVE DABBLER (original)

**Hook:** Fulling Mill Comp, sizes 10 and 12
**Tail:** Natural pheasant tail
**Rib:** Gold wire
**Body:** Golden olive seal's fur
**Body hackle:** Palmered golden olive hen
**Wing:** Cloaked bronze mallard

## CLARET DABBLER (original)

**Hook:** Fulling Mill Comp, sizes 10 and 12
**Tail:** Natural or dyed claret pheasant tail
**Rib:** Gold wire
**Body:** Dark claret seal's fur
**Body hackle:** Palmered claret hen
**Wing:** Cloaked bronze mallard

## UV STRAGGLE DABBLER

**Hook:** Size 12 double
**Tail:** Pheasant tail – natural or dyed to suit
**Body:** 1.5mm UV straggle, Synergy is best
**Hackle:** Colour to suit
**Wing:** Cloaked bronze mallard
**Cheeks:** Optional – JC splits, natural or dyed to suit

country, scale them down with a minimalist approach and go 'skinny'.

Strange how a conventional black-bodied Dabbler doesn't do a lot to excite wild brown trout whereas a Silver Dabbler with a black hackle running through it really seems to stamp their card, certainly in springtime in Ireland.

My own personal favourite in the world of Dabblers, although it only has a part-silver body in its make-up, is my humble Peter Ross Dabbler. This one works for me throughout the whole season and I reckon it's the best middle-dropper wet fly I've ever had.

Between ugly things on the cast for rainbows, just give it a swim late season on Rutland, or if it's wild browns, try it between a top-dropper bumble and whatever you fancy on the point. Size 12 seems to fit the bill best for both species. For springtime fishing I prefer it tied with a palmered black hackle, and later in the season I'd side with a heavily black-centred badger-hackled version, jungle cock cheeks being optional.

But hey! Just because wild brownies are the quarry doesn't mean that a little bit of synthetic doesn't work for them.

Certainly on Mask, Melvin, Vyrnwy and Brenig early season, I've been pretty successful with micro-UV Straggle-bodied Dabblers tied on doubles and fished as an out-and-out point fly.

Mask is peaty and the flash will help stir up interest, whereas Melvin is mostly about shoaling sonaghan and greedy competition for food – first find the shoal and they will do the rest. Best UV Straggle Dabblers for these two loughs are black and gold, black and silver, claret or, believe it or not but I have it on good authority, at times on Melvin the black-finned trout are partial to something with a peach-coloured body.

Being an old purist, I find it hard not to get some fur or feather into the dressing at some stage, and one pattern that utilises both traditional and modern very effectively for me has a UV body overdressed with a long mobile hen hackle in the 'colour of the day' prior to tying in the wing. The best colours are golden olive and various shades of claret, but I always find space in the fly box for magenta and hot orange.

There are times when my early season trip to tackle duck-fly-feeding trout on Lough Corrib is knocked out of kilter by the Irish weather, wind being the main problem. 'Figure of eighting' epoxy buzzers in a blow is no fun, so we are often forced to move away from the deeper 'holes' and on to the shallows in search of wet-fly sport. The best early season Dabbler I have found to put a bend in the rod was given me by that old Corrib stalwart, Frank Reilly and that's the Silver Dabbler.

Nothing beats experience
when it comes to locating
grayling in coloured water.
The ability to read the water
is essential.

# PRETTY POLYS

Simon Kidd goes 'upside down' and describes a method of
tying and fishing nymphs to reach the right spots for grayling

Choosing the right size and weight of fly can be crucial to achieving correct depth and presentation – in addition to the pattern itself!

Some people talk about using 'sacrificial' flies, such as we – the England World Team – witnessed in Slovakia in 2004, where heavily weighted lumps of lead with hooks protruding, loosely passing as flies, were lobbed into the river.

They were designed to sink an accompanying nymph to the bottom and to be effective in the heavy flows of the Tatra Mountain tributaries, which indeed they were.

Personally, where possible I prefer to use a fly that is not sacrificial but is one that will catch fish consistently as well as deliver the other flies on the leader to the area required. In this way you have to be increasing the chances of success.

One such favourite has been a combination of the Peeping Caddis I first fished on Devon rivers in my school days and the Polyfeitus introduced to me by John Barnes in Norway. This I call the Peeping Poly and I can use brass or the more-modern tungsten to provide weight and depth. Darrel Martin refers to Branco Gasparin's Polyfeitus in his book, entitled 'Micropatterns'. I now have several favourite variations, but the Peeping Poly will remain a strong favourite for me on many venues.

## FIRST, FIND YOUR FISH

Wherever we choose to fish, locating the right spots is imperative if we are to catch fish – 'first, find your fish' being that number-one priority. When you're after winter grayling, especially in waters such as the chalkstreams of the south where they can be visible at times, the job of location can be quite easy. Keeping out of sight can present the main challenge!

When the waters are coloured with run-off from rain or snow melt or, as with many of our freestone rivers, where there is a tinge of natural colour, the fish are very well protected and camouflaged by the natural contours and features of the river.

Here, initial location can be a much harder task. Of course it is easier if the odd fish decides to rise and give its location away but, otherwise, having a good, initial setup in which we have strong confidence is a sound way to start prospecting. For me, this often employs a two or three-nymph set-up, frequently with a Poly on the point.

Experience and repeat visits, especially if you are disciplined enough to keep a log, will help to locate regular fish-holding spots at certain times of the year, of course. Once having successfully located the fish, fly choice and control at the correct depth will prove crucial to success.

Leading the line initially, reducing line drag, can help the point flies reach the bottom quicker.

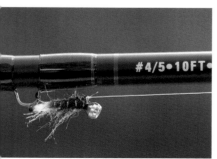

An 'aerated' fly box on a lanyard holds used flies and helps to dry them before being put away.

A 10ft length for a 4/5-wt rod provides control as well as delicacy.

Reading the creases, obstacles, ebbs and flows can provide invaluable clues and, here, having the right equipment and approach will reduce time spent searching.

Clear chalkstreams offer huge benefits, for here everything is so visible that not only can the fish be easily seen but your fly presentation and depth can also. Therefore, clear water can provide an ideal practice ground for learning techniques.

However, you don't have to visit a chalkstream to find clear water because the River Wye and many others can also be very clear at times. Remaining concealed from the view of fish here can still prove as important as being able to see and understand what fish and flies are doing beneath the water.

Unfortunately, there are times, as on our visit to the Wye on this occasion, where one is as good as blindfolded to subsurface activity, through the coloured and murky water following recent rainfall. Here, the techniques tried in clear water, learning how the flies move and sink and how the fish respond in relation to certain activity, really comes into play.

## LONG ROD, LIGHT LINE

Very often, I will fish one or two Polys, the first on the point and the next (smaller) on the middle dropper. In shallower water, the middle fly may be more effective and give me more flexibility if the depths vary from beat to beat.

My first dropper is tied in about five feet from the tip of the fly line or braid. I use a dropper of about four inches normally and then another fly at least 20 inches below. The final point fly, which unfailingly is the Poly, I tie about another 20 inches beyond the middle dropper.

In very difficult water I would drop down to just two flies... or even one. Four to 6lb fluorocarbon is usually adequate, although I have been forced to go finer and 2lb tippet has been necessary with smaller flies on occasion. As with most nymphing methods on the river, I prefer to use a 10ft 4/5-wt rod for best control around the eddies and for the best drag-free reach I can achieve.

Having the heaviest fly on the point is the favourite way for me to detect the slightest movement, as all the flies will line up and takes will be detected instantly. The Polyfeitus' pattern offers much less of an opportunity to snag the bottom, compared to most of the other conventionally tied patterns, as it is trotted along the bottom with the hook point uppermost.

## TYING THE POLYFEITUS

This range of flies has not only helped me to fish other patterns more effectively in all water conditions but has also caught fish in river

### POLYFEITUS BLACK
**Hook:** AP 31180, sizes 10 to 14
**Silk:** Black
**Tail:** Partridge
**Body:** Hare's ear/SLF mix
**Rib:** Thin gold wire
**Hackle:** Partridge
**Bead:** Faceted tungsten (faceted to distinguish tungsten from brass)

Clear water can be of benefit to the novice. Watching fish behaviour goes a long way to understanding how to fish for them.

1 Tie a bent pin and bead securely on the top of the hook. Adding lead for additional weight, bind thoroughly and secure it with a dab of superglue.

2 Tie in the wool tail (singed with a match), and three strands of Angel Hair, snipping off two ends and leaving one long.

3 Loosely, tie in the tail hackle running towards the eye of the hook. Stroke the fibres back and tie over so that it lays flat around the wool tail.

4 Stroke the fibres back and tie over so that it lays flat around the wool tail. Next, apply the dubbing, covering all of the exposed thread.

5 Rib the dubbed body with the remaining strand of Angel Hair and tie it off, removing the excess. Whip finish around the pin and secure it with varnish.

systems in virtually every country I have so far been lucky enough to fish. The profile of the fly helps it to sink or, more appropriately, 'dive' to the bottom, plus the weight and size are easily combined to match the water depth and condition.

Colour can be an important consideration but, to me, the profile, size and orientation of the fly are equally crucial factors. Colour can also play a part when fish that have become familiar with certain patterns need a change in order to bring about renewed action.

## DEPTH AND TRICKY FISH

Grayling can often be seen sitting close to the bottom in clear water, unfazed by an assortment of objects coming through the water. Spooked or just not feeding, these fish can be encouraged to respond to the 'induced take' if proving really difficult. Presenting the right flies at the right depths and speeds is the only way to glean any sort of reaction on these occasions.

The induced take is an exaggerated movement, usually obtained by gently lifting the rod tip at a timely point, either upwards or across the flow, to which the fish is instinctively drawn to grab the disappearing item. This simple but effective method can convert many half-interested enquiries into solid takes.

First and foremost, however, the fly must reach the depth at which the fish will respond and this often means putting your target flies right into or below the location where the fish is sitting. Flies such as the Polyfeitus serve to do just that. If fish are 'on the fin' and feeding, they may be looking up; consequently, they may respond to a fly passing above them. However, if they have seen you or are not feeding but are merely resting or even preoccupied by foraging along the bottom, then anything remotely distant from the fish, even just above them, can have no effect whatsoever.

In winter months this can require planting the flies right on the bottom, where the flow

## POLYFEITUS NATURAL

**Hook:** AP 31180, sizes 10 to 14
**Silk:** Brown or rust
**Tail:** Partridge
**Body:** Hare's ear dub
**Rib:** Thin gold wire
**Hackle:** Partridge
**Bead:** Faceted tungsten (faceted to distinguish tungsten from brass)

## PEEPING POLY

**Hook:** Tiemco 103 BL11-15
**Silk:** Red tying silk
**Tail:** Tinged polyester/wool and three strands of Angel Hair
**Tail hackle:** Grizzle or cree cock
**Body:** Possum/SLF mix
**Rib:** Angel hair
**Bead:** Silver or gold brass or tungsten

is slower than the main current above. This bottom couple of inches of drag-affected water moves fractionally slower than that above it. The higher in the water, of course, the less resistance is caused from the riverbed, resulting in the upper layers of water flowing much faster.

The tying of the flies can provide some movement – the 'trigger points' as far as I am concerned. With the Peeping Poly this could be said of the bead, the burnt-wool tail or the twinkling Angel Hair and feather fibre. Furthermore, the fact that the hook will be turned uppermost in its natural orientation presents a better chance of hooking the grayling in its characteristically large upper lip.

To be most effective using this technique, you must achieve the slowest and the most controlled movement possible of the flies near the bottom of the river. This means that where the line breaks the surface, it needs to move more slowly than the surface water around it. At times, it becomes almost instinctive to anticipate that a take will occur when getting it absolutely right. You should feel directly in control and that is the way it should stay to be effective.

Holding the fly line back against the current can achieve this effect, but the reverse can almost work even better at the start of the presentation. By leading the line downriver initially, you can actually reduce the drag on

the line beneath the water. This, in turn, allows the flies to sink more naturally under their own weight and to reach the depth they need to be in order to work.

If you allow any drag, the flies will be whipped up clear of the bottom by the current above them. This can produce an induced-take effect initially, but as the water resistance below tugs at the leader and the line trying to force the flies downriver you end up holding them off the bottom and they may never reach the right depth at all.

Through winter months, grayling can prove a great quarry for the fly angler and this method has produced plenty for me over the years. While balmy summer days after trout have been parked in the memory until another spring, grayling are active throughout winter months as they build up to their main spawning period early the following year.

They will frequently rise for short periods during the day too. For this reason I always carry another rod equipped with dries, or a team of nymphs with a small spider or wet fly on the top dropper. When not visible on the surface, they can provide great sport and will demand a range of skills using heavier nymphs. They can build into large shoals too and, although the better fish are often less gregarious, some great fishing can be had whatever the weather.

## RIVER WYE FACT FILE

The recent hard work and developments by the Wye and Usk Foundation has meant that even more beautiful stretches of water are now available to the casual grayling and trout angler.

"Grayling are active throughout winter as they build up to their main spawning period early the following year."

Having a wading staff is essential in waters such as the Wye, where drop-offs and boulders are just waiting to get you. This is made doubly dangerous when the water is coloured.

When playing a grayling, keeping it off the surface by holding the rod to the side – especially when fishing barbless – will help reduce the number of lost fish.

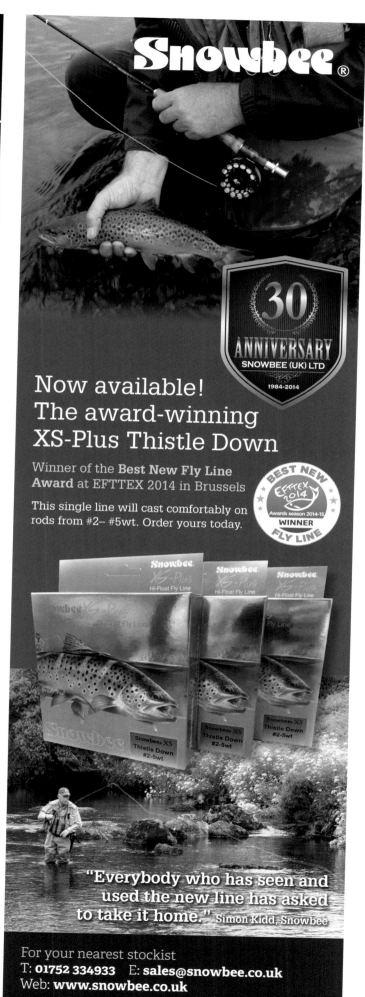

# DEE DEVIL

Peacock herl – a magical material if ever there was one – combined with red is a marriage made in heaven when it comes to grayling flies. This tasty-looking morsel is a real eye-catcher and the grayling – and quite often trout – are more than happy to take it! Fish it in a team of three nymphs, Czech-nymph style, for best results.

**Hook:** Standard grub, size 10
**Thread:** Black
**Tag:** Glo-Brite No3
**Body:** Peacock herl
**Rib:** Med copper wire
**Cheeks:** Red holographic
**Hackle:** Partridge
**Bead:** 3mm black tungsten

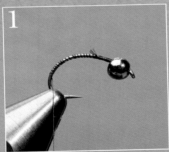

**1** Place the bead onto the hook and put the hook in the vice before running on tying thread.

**2** At the ear of the hook attach a doubled length of floss, wind down to create a butt and back up before securing and trimming waste.

**3** At the back of the hook attach two strands of peacock herl and the copper wire ribbing material.

**4** Wind the herl up to the thorax in touching turns, secure and trim. Do the same with the rib but in open turns in the opposite direction.

**5** Attach the holo either side of the shank and attach some more herl. Wind this up and pull the holo up as cheeks.

**6** Tie in the hackle by the tips, wind around the shank twice, secure and trim. Attach more herl, whip finish with thread for a neat head area.